THE GREATEST BURGER EVER SOLD

The Greatest
Burger
Ever Sold

and other sketches

NICK MCIVOR

Illustrated by Russell Davies

MINSTREL
Eastbourne

First published 1989

Cover design by Russell Davies

British Library Cataloguing in Publication Data

McIvor, Nick
    The greatest burger ever sold
    I. Title
    822'.914

    ISBN 1–85424–037–4 (Minstrel)
        0–7324–0423–1 (Albatross)

Published in Australia by Albatross Books
PO Box 320, Sutherland, NSW 2232

Printed in Great Britain for
Minstrel, an imprint of Monarch Publications Ltd
1 St Anne's Road, Eastbourne, E Sussex BN21 3UN by
Richard Clay Ltd, Bungay, Suffolk
Typeset by J&L Composition Ltd, Filey, North Yorkshire

CONTENTS

FOREWORD

'Give me something new for Christmas' is not just something irritating children say. Every news editor, TV producer, radio boss and, dare I say, vicar, has spent many hours trying to come up with a new angle on this much-loved story.

What Nick McIvor has done is to provide both the drama group and the casual reader with a fascinating series of sketches and insights into the New Testament story. The contents of this book could amuse, provoke, entertain, challenge or disturb you. If it does all five, as it did me, it will have succeeded admirably.

Simon Mayo

Note on
PERFORMING RIGHTS

The copyright holder's permission should always be obtained before performing any play or sketch. Licences normally refer to a specific performance but, for the material in this book, a fee of £15.00 guarantees the perpetual right to perform any of the sketches in any context or combination. It does not confer the right to reproduce the text in any fashion (see publisher's copyright note), and acknowledgements should mention title, author and publisher.

Licences may be obtained from:

The Greatest Burger Ever Sold
PO Box 1686
London NW6 3EJ

All cheques should be made payable to 'The Greatest Burger Ever Sold'. Applications should be made in the name of the church, group or individual that intends to present the material. Only one such licence is needed for any one group of performers, but licences are not transferrable.

The above refers to amateur productions (with paying or non-paying audiences). A separate application should be made to the same address by any fully professional company wishing to use the material, and will involve the payment of royalties on box-office takings. All cassette recording, radio, television, video and film rights are reserved.

1

PROLOGUE

Scene:
A street in Nazareth. The REPORTER is smartly dressed and talking directly to the audience.

REPORTER:
Jesus, son of Joseph, was born into a working-class family deep in the Empire's east end. A carpenter by trade, he spent most of his life in the small provincial town of Nazareth and, in spite of doubts about his parentage, he was accepted by the local community. Then, at the age of thirty, everything changed, because that was the age when he revealed his astonishing gifts as public speaker, doctor, and large-scale caterer. Soon he was travelling the country preaching, teaching, and arranging meals for up to 5,000 at a sitting. It was said that he had developed a process for instantaneously fermenting bathwater into vintage claret, and some of his medical cures have been described as little short of miraculous. Indeed, he exposed a number of quack physicians, after showing patients they had pronounced dead to be merely unwell.

But there was another, darker side to this man's nature. In spite of his great generosity—he never demanded payment for any of these services—he was politically subversive, and it was these radical politics, plus his claim to be a close relative of some local deity, that finally led to his arrest and execution.

However, the story doesn't end there. A few days after the execution his body disappeared, and there were reports that he had been seen eating, speaking and walking through locked doors. Unfortunately, many of the eyewitnesses have themselves been executed, and are therefore unavailable for comment, leaving us to ponder the question: Who was Jesus of Nazareth?

'IT'D MAKE A LOVELY CARD...'

2

WHILE SHEPHERDS WATCHED

Scene:
  A hillside. A lone shepherd is talking directly to the audience.

SHEPHERD:
Hello! My name's Nathanael, and I'm a shepherd. Because of this, I'm known as 'Nathanael the Shepherd'.

In case you're wondering where the others are, they're all running about Bethlehem, looking for a baby in a horse-trough. Not the usual place for a baby, I know, but that's where the man in the nightie said he'd be.

It's been one of those nights.

I knew we were in for trouble when Benjamin started complaining about his feet. When Benjamin starts complaining about his feet, it can only mean two things, either he's been jogging without his sandals again, or it's going to be one of those nights.

Then we found out we had to count the sheep again. Everybody knows the problem with counting sheep in the middle of the night, and I thought I'd come up with quite a crafty solution. What we did was to count ten sheep on the hour every hour when we were on duty, and it seemed to be working very well. I began to get suspicious last week when the total got to 13,000, and tonight the news came—start again.

Well, we'd just started again for the fifth time when the man in the nightie turned up. Of course, now I know it wasn't a man in a nightie, but when you meet someone in the middle of the night wearing a funny costume and talking about a baby, you don't instantly jump to the conclusion that it's an angel. I thought it was his child and he'd been out celebrating. Then all his mates turned up and began singing. He called them the heavenly host, and at first I thought it must be a private association, 'cos they were all wearing nighties too. Then I realised they weren't people in nighties. The singing was a clue, 'cos we don't have any choirs like that around here, but I think what clinched it was the fact that they were all 250 feet up in the air.

I must say we all found this a wee bit disconcerting. Benjamin began whimpering about his feet again, Philip pretended he was a sheep and tried to sneak off down the hill, and the only reason Nathan didn't do anything was because he'd passed out. Then this angel told us not to be frightened—very reassuring— and said that there was a very important baby in a stable, under a star, and that we should visit him. Well, that seemed a bit vague so we asked him which star, and he pointed out this great big one I hadn't seen before. It turned out he'd brought it with him, very nice too. Anyway, that's where the others have gone.

They took one of the sheep with them. That was Philip's idea. He said if it was somebody that important we ought to give him a present, and when you're stuck on a hillside at three o'clock in the morning, the choice isn't great.

I got left behind to keep an eye on the rest of the flock, and to come up with another crafty way of counting them—and I've done it. The secret is, not to count the sheep at all, just count the legs and divide by four. Now I know what you're thinking. You're thinking, 'There's an awful lot of legs out there, you're never going to count them all at one go.' Quite right. What I'm going to do is count ten legs on the hour, every hour I'm on duty ... [*He leaves*]

3

IN THE INN

For children, indoors. Read Appendix 3, 'Working with Children', before doing this sketch.

Characters:
NARRATOR played by adult
EMPEROR imperious, played by NARRATOR
INNKEEPER harassed, played by NARRATOR
CROWD minimum of three plus
SHEPHERD yokel, part of CROWD until inn scene
WISE MAN academic, part of CROWD until inn scene
JOSEPH anxious father, part of CROWD until inn scene

Scene:
A street in Bethlehem, then Caesar's Palace, then an inn. There should be some chairs at the side of the stage for use in the restaurant scene, but no other set is required. At the beginning of the sketch, only the NARRATOR is present. If there are more children, ignore the numbering and let them take it in turns to speak.

NARRATOR:
Bethlehem, a sleepy little town, just south of Jerusalem, was seething with visitors.

[CROWD *enter and 'bustle'*]

But what were they doing there? Were they sightseeing?

[CROWD *shake their heads*]

Were they doing business?

[CROWD *shake their heads again*]

Were they visiting?

[CROWD *shake their heads yet again*]

Then what were they doing?

[CROWD *arrange themselves in a line, and one of them starts counting the rest*]

Yes, they were there being counted. I'll explain: Bethlehem was in Judea, and Judea was part of the Roman Empire. Now, about a year ago, the Emperor had asked a question:

[CROWD *become* COURTIERS, *and each goes down on one knee.* NARRATOR *becomes* EMPEROR]

EMPEROR:
How many people live in my empire?

1ST COURTIER:
Ah, a good question, Great Caesar.

2ND COURTIER:
A very good question.

3RD COURTIER:
The best question I have heard in a long time.

EMPEROR:
Well, what is the answer?

4TH COURTIER:
Well, it's difficult to say exactly.

EMPEROR:
Roughly, then.

5TH COURTIER:
Um, it's pretty difficult to say roughly.

EMPEROR:
Well, very roughly!

6TH COURTIER:
Still not easy.

EMPEROR:
Does anybody have any idea what the answer is?
    [COURTIERS *look embarrassed*]

EMPEROR:
In that case, we will have a census!

1ST COURTIER:
Brilliant!

2ND COURTIER:
Inspired!

3RD COURTIER:
Astounding!
    [*Pause*]

4TH COURTIER:
What's a census?

EMPEROR:
Every man in every province of the Roman Empire
will return to the town of his birth, and be counted!
    [JOSEPH, SHEPHERD *and* WISE MAN *leave the stage.*
    Remaining members of CROWD *collect chairs, and*
    become INN CUSTOMERS *sitting at imaginary tables.*
    EMPEROR *becomes* NARRATOR *again*]

NARRATOR:
Which is why there were so many visitors in
Bethlehem. Now, in one particular inn, things were
getting a little out of hand. The guests were sleeping
four to a room, they were in the loft, they were in the
basement, they were in the corridors, they were even
in the stables, and the restaurant was in chaos:
    [NARRATOR *becomes* INNKEEPER]

1ST CUSTOMER:
Waiter! Waiter! More wine!

2ND CUSTOMER:
Can I have the bill, please?

3RD CUSTOMER:
What's happened to my soup?

INNKEEPER:
One at a time, please! Now, who wanted more wine?

1ST CUSTOMER:
I did!

3RD CUSTOMER:
So do I!

[*JOSEPH enters at a run*]

JOSEPH:
Blankets!

INNKEEPER:
I'm afraid you'll have to wait your turn!

JOSEPH:
But my wife's having a baby!

INNKEEPER:
What?

1ST CUSTOMER:
What's going on here?

2ND CUSTOMER:
I didn't think it was that kind of place.

3RD CUSTOMER:
It's the last time I'm coming here.

INNKEEPER:
The linen cupboard under the stairs!

[*JOSEPH runs off*]

INNKEEPER:
Now, who was next?

1ST CUSTOMER:
I was!

2ND CUSTOMER:
No, I was!

3RD CUSTOMER:
I still haven't got my soup!

INNKEEPER:
[*To* 2ND CUSTOMER] Right, you wanted a bill. [*He tears off a piece of paper from his pad, and hands it to him*]
    [*JOSEPH runs in again, now carrying blankets*]

JOSEPH:
Hot water!

INNKEEPER:
What! [*Sees* JOSEPH. *Points*] In the kitchen, through that door on the left. Now get out!
    [*JOSEPH runs off*]

INNKEEPER:
Now, wine.

3RD CUSTOMER:
And my soup!

INNKEEPER:
And soup.
    [*SHEPHERD enters with lamb under his arm*]

SHEPHERD:
Evening!
    [*SHEEP bleats*]

INNKEEPER:
What the ... ?

SHEPHERD:
Perhaps you can help me ...

INNKEEPER:
[*Outraged*] What is that you've got there?

SHEPHERD:
Oh, it's just a little lamb.

INNKEEPER:
It's an animal!

SHEPHERD:
Aye, now ...
    [*SHEEP bleats*]

INNKEEPER:
You can't bring that in here!
SHEPHERD:
Oh, don't worry, it'll be all right.
INNKEEPER:
People are eating in here!
SHEPHERD:
I was just wondering if there was ...
INNKEEPER:
Get out!
SHEPHERD:
I just wanted to know if there's a baby about the place?
INNKEEPER:
In the stable. Now get that thing out of here!
  [SHEEP *bleats. Nasty 'slopping' noise follows.*
  SHEPHERD *exits*]
INNKEEPER:
[*Looks at the imaginary mess on the floor*] Barnabas! Clean this up! This town's gone mad!
3RD CUSTOMER:
Where is my soup?
INNKEEPER:
On it's way! [*He starts to go for soup*]
  [WISE MAN *enters carrying a jug of liquid*]
WISE MAN:
Ahem! Excuse me!
INNKEEPER:
We're full up!
WISE MAN:
I'm looking for ...
INNKEEPER:
[*He has become aware of a strange smell*] What's that smell?

WISE MAN:
Oh, just the embalming fluid.
INNKEEPER:
Embalming fluid! In a restaurant. Leave!
WISE MAN:
I'm looking for a young child ...
INNKEEPER:
In the stable, now go!
WISE MAN:
Thanks a lot. [*He starts to go. Looks down*] Bit of a mess on the floor here ... I think you'd better clear it up.
    [*WISE MAN exits*]
3RD CUSTOMER:
Can I have my soup!
INNKEEPER:
Yes. Right away!
    [*INNKEEPER exits, and becomes NARRATOR again*]
3RD CUSTOMER:
What a piece of nonsense!
1ST CUSTOMER:
I won't be coming back.
2ND CUSTOMER:
I've never seen anything like it.
3RD CUSTOMER:
All these people just wandering in and out.
NARRATOR:
And while the customers complained and the innkeeper tried to keep his temper, a child was born in the stable. But apart from his parents, a few shepherds, and some odd foreign travellers, nobody noticed.

'...THEN THE MAN WITH THE HALO AND THE NIGHTIE BEGAN SINGING...'

4

MATERNITY WARD

Scene:

A stable. JOSEPH is on the telephone. There is no point in filling the stage with straw and other stable-like trappings, as these will simply draw the audience's attention to the incongruity of having JOSEPH using a telephone in the first place. All that is required is a table for the phone, and the telephone itself. JOSEPH is nervous and should stand throughout. If you are going to perform this sketch, or indeed any of the monologues, it's a good idea to read Appendix 2, 'Monologues', first.

JOSEPH:

Hello, Mother, it's Joseph ... Your son ... Yes, I know it's been a long time since I last rang. I'm afraid I've been rather busy ... [*JOSEPH looks bored*] Yes, Mother, I'm still here ... Oh I'm fine, fine ... Mary? She's fine. Mother, I think I ought to come and see you sometime soon ... Oh, it's no trouble. You see, I'm actually in Bethlehem for the census ... Ah, well of course I would have stayed with you but, um, I knew how busy you'd be, and thought you'd have enough on your hands without the three of us turning up ... Did I say three? Mary, me, and the donkey, that is ... We've got a room, well, more of a stable really ... Oh now, Mother, don't get upset. I only said 'stable' because it's full of straw and animals and [*He sniffs the air suspiciously*] things. No, what I should have said was 'stable-like building', extremely stable-like. Mother, are you sitting? ... Well, it's just that I've got something to tell you, and I really do think you'd be better to hear it in a seated position. Ready? ... I'm a father— only I'm not. What I mean is that I've got a son—in a manner of speaking. What I'm trying to say is that Mary's had a baby boy, which is, I suppose, in some sense mine, if not actually my own. In so many words. If you get my drift. Mother? [*There is no reply*] Mother? [*Still no reply*] Mother? [*No reply again*] Mother, are you still there? ... [*He holds the phone at arm's length as if he is being shouted at*] Yes, you are, aren't you? ... Well ... [*His mother won't let him get a word in edgeways*] If you'd just let me explain ... [*Shouting*] Well, what would you do if your fiancée told you she'd just been discussing family planning with an archangel? ... Of course I didn't believe her. At least, not until I'd talked it over with him myself ... [*Defensively*] Yes, I know it doesn't take an angel to make a baby ... Of course I remember what you told me about the birds and the bees! How could I forget? I was ten years old at the time, and I spent the next two months in terror of being stung by a wasp in case I got pregnant! [*JOSEPH looks across the room and sees somebody entering*] Look, I'll have to go, we've got guests ... [*Peering over at them*] Four shepherds, three oriental diplomats, and a baby lamb. Give my love to father. [*He hangs up and exits briskly*]

5

NATIVITY SCENE

Characters:
  PHOTOGRAPHER sharply dressed, a bit flash
  JOSEPH the puzzled father
  MARY the slightly cynical mother
Scene:
  A stable. The only essential prop is a broom, but it
  would help to have some rubbish scattered around
  the floor: straw would be ideal.

  JOSEPH and the PHOTOGRAPHER enter. The PHOTO-
  GRAPHER has several cameras around his neck and a
  bag of extra equipment in his hand.

PHOTOGRAPHER:
[*Looking around*] This is terrific, Joseph, just terrific!
JOSEPH:
[*Incredulous*] You think so?
PHOTOGRAPHER:
Oh, absolutely. I mean, just look around you!
JOSEPH:
[*Looking*] It's a stable.

PHOTOGRAPHER:
It's a stable, yes, but it's more than that. It's so full
of ...

JOSEPH:
Dirt.

PHOTOGRAPHER:
Not quite the word I had in mind.

JOSEPH:
[*Helpfully*] Filth?

PHOTOGRAPHER:
I was thinking more of ...

JOSEPH:
The animals?

PHOTOGRAPHER:
No ...

JOSEPH:
The damp?

PHOTOGRAPHER:
The atmosphere, Joseph, this place reeks of atmosphere and ...

JOSEPH:
Cow droppings.

PHOTOGRAPHER:
[*Sniffs the air*] Yes, well, it all adds to the general
ambience.

JOSEPH:
And makes a terrible mess of your shoes. [*He looks
down at the* PHOTOGRAPHER'*s feet*]

PHOTOGRAPHER:
[*Laughing self-consciously*] Yes, I'm sure it does. [*He
catches* JOSEPH'*s gaze and follows it to his own feet*]
Ah, yes. [*He wipes his foot surreptitiously on the
floor*] Well, we'll clear all this up before we start.
Now, whereabouts is your lovely lady wife?

JOSEPH:

[*Calling*] Mary! Mary! We've got a visitor.

MARY:

[*Enters carrying a 'child' wrapped in an old blanket. She is mildly irritated*] Who is it now?

JOSEPH:

This is Gordon, Mary.

MARY:

You've come to see the baby?

PHOTOGRAPHER:

Yes, how did you know?

MARY:

Same as all the others. And what have you brought? So far we've had half a dozen gold teaspoons, a bottle of perfume, a small sheep and a jug of embalming fluid.

PHOTOGRAPHER:

I've just brought a camera I'm afraid.

MARY:

[*Sighs*] A camera.

PHOTOGRAPHER:

[*Nodding*] Mmmm.

MARY:

Thank you very much, it's just what we needed. [*She takes the camera and starts to leave*]

PHOTOGRAPHER:

[*He still has the camera around his neck and is being dragged after her*] No ... no ... I'm here to take some photographs!

MARY:

[*Stopping*] Photographs? [*She gives the camera back to the PHOTOGRAPHER and goes over to JOSEPH*] Joseph, did you arrange this?

JOSEPH:

Yes, I didn't think you'd mind.

MARY:
I told you, we can't afford a photographer.

PHOTOGRAPHER:
Oh no, you don't have to pay. I just want to take a few library shots.

JOSEPH:
[*Confused*] I thought you wanted to take them in the stable?

PHOTOGRAPHER:
No, I mean ... look, be a good chap and clear up some of this rubbish, will you?

JOSEPH:
Clear it up?

PHOTOGRAPHER:
That's right. I mean, it's not going to make a very attractive set of pictures if there's dirt and ... you know ... 'business' about the place.

JOSEPH:
[*Reluctantly fetches the broom and starts sweeping up*]

PHOTOGRAPHER:
Now, Mary, what we're trying to capture here is a sense of the family coping in adversity.

MARY:
You mean like a baby in one arm and a dead rat in the other?

PHOTOGRAPHER:
Well, I don't think we want to overdo the adversity. Now, do you have anything to put him in?

MARY:
What sort of thing did you have in mind?

PHOTOGRAPHER:
Oh, I don't know ... a little cot or something?

MARY:
[*Incredulous*] In a stable?

PHOTOGRAPHER:
I suppose not. Well, never mind.

MARY:
We were using the manger as a sort of bed.

PHOTOGRAPHER:
[*Enthusiastically*] What, the thing the animals eat from? How quaint.

MARY:
[*Pointing*] That's it, over there.

PHOTOGRAPHER:
[*Less keen*] It's a bit dirty, isn't it?

MARY:
[*Shaking her head*] Cows, they're such messy eaters.

PHOTOGRAPHER:
Let's just have you holding the baby for the moment. [*Pointing at the blanket*] Is that all you've got to wrap him in?

MARY:
I'm afraid so.

PHOTOGRAPHER:
Yes, well we can't have that. [*He reaches inside his bag and pulls out a spotlessly clean sheet*] Use this. [*To* JOSEPH, *who has been sweeping up all this time*] Finished, Joseph?

JOSEPH:
Just this bit.

PHOTOGRAPHER:
That's enough, we'll be able to keep everything else out of shot.

MARY:
[*Looking around*] It's a bit dingy, isn't it?

PHOTOGRAPHER:
With this film it'll look as bright as day. In fact, if I get the exposure just right, we should have a nice warm glow round the baby's head. [*He positions* MARY *and*

takes some pictures] Lovely. Now, Joseph, if you'd like to step into the frame.

JOSEPH:

[*JOSEPH has been watching*] What frame?

PHOTOGRAPHER:

Stand beside your wife.

JOSEPH: [*Stands beside MARY awkwardly, with the broom still in his hand*]

PHOTOGRAPHER:

I don't think we want to see that. [*He takes away the broom*] Now Joseph, look at your son.

JOSEPH:

Ah, well he's not exactly my son ...

MARY:

[*Nudges him sharply*]

PHOTOGRAPHER:

What?

JOSEPH:

Nothing ... yes, look at him [*He stares intensely at the 'baby', frowning with concentration*]

PHOTOGRAPHER:

That's not quite what I had in mind. Could you look at him in wonder?

JOSEPH:

Look at him and wonder what?

PHOTOGRAPHER:

No, in wonder.

JOSEPH:

How do you mean?

PHOTOGRAPHER:

[*Exasperated*] Look at the spot on the end of his nose!

JOSEPH:

[*Peering at the 'baby's' face*] What spot?

PHOTOGRAPHER:

[*Taking pictures*] Lovely. Well, we'll leave it at that

for the time being. I'll come back later in the week to get some of him in the manger.

MARY:

I thought you said it was too dirty.

PHOTOGRAPHER:

Oh no, not that one, we'll bring one of our own. Thanks for all your help. [*He starts to go*] Cheerio! [*He leaves*]

MARY:

What was all that about?

JOSEPH:

I don't know. He just said he wanted some pictures. [*Remembering something*] Oh, he did give me this. [*He takes out a calling card and gives it to* MARY]

MARY:

[*Reading the card*] Gordon Fraser greeting cards.

    [MARY *looks at* JOSEPH; *they both shrug and leave*]

6

MASTERCLASS

Scene:
  A classroom. A teacher's desk on stage. The SCHOOL-MISTRESS enters. She carries a briefcase.

SCHOOLMISTRESS:
Good morning, class ... [*She sees the blackboard*]
Who wrote that silly word on the blackboard? Come
on, own up ... Clean it off, Simon, I'll speak to you at
break-time ... And we can do without the funny
noises, Philip!

  Now something very exciting is happening today,
can anyone guess what it is? ... No, Matthew, I'm not
retiring. James? ... No, the Romans aren't going to
be overthrown and replaced by a new government
founded on the laws of Moses. But that's a very good
answer. Anybody else? ... One more noise like that,
Philip, and you can stand outside the room. Today,
we've got a new boy joining the class, now he's called
Jesus, and he's going to be a little late because he has
to come all the way from Nazareth. Has anyone here
ever been to Nazareth? ... Bartholomew, tell the class

what it's like ... Don't be silly, Bartholomew, of course it doesn't smell!

Now, I want you all to be on your best behaviour when Jesus arrives, because I've heard he's a very good boy ... Being good isn't boring, Timothy ... No, it's not. Anyway, how would you know, you've never tried it.

Right, today we're looking at the story of Jonah, does anybody here know anything about Jonah? ... Yes, Bartholomew? ... Why did Jonah smell, Bartholomew? ... because he spent three days inside a fish. Thank you, Bartholomew, I'm sure we'll all remember that. [*Glancing across the room*] Put it down, John. Philip, what do you know about him? ... He was a prophet, yes, very good, anybody else? Yes? ... He went on a boat, yes, and [*She catches a glimpse of somebody else*] John, put it down! ... And there was a storm, that's right. Now, what happened during the storm? [*She catches sight of John again*] John, no! ... I don't care if you do want to baptise him, you're not to pour any water over James! Now can we please get back to Jonah!

So far, we'd agreed that he was a prophet who ran away on a boat and was caught in a storm ... What do you mean how do we know? We know because it was all written down ... in the Scriptures ... in the Book of Jonah ... of course it's not made up ... Oh for goodness sake, Thomas, it's true!

What is it now, Bartholomew? ... Look, I'm beginning to get very tired of this. Simon doesn't smell ... no, he doesn't ... no, he doesn't ... [*She sniffs*] Well, anyway, what's wrong with fish?

So, there was Jonah in the middle of a terrible storm, the wind was howling and the waves were crashing over the deck ... [*She winces*] All right, John, what was that for? ... When I want a demonstration of waves crashing over the deck, I'll ask. Now stand in the corner.

The rest of you are to imagine yourselves standing on the deck of the boat with the wind howling and the waves· crashing ... No, you wouldn't be swept away ... Because, well, you just wouldn't. Now I want you to imagine yourself standing on that deck, and I want you to draw a picture of what you see. John, that's a fire bucket ... Just put it down ... Come in. Ah hello, Jesus. Children, this is the new boy I was telling you about—John, no! [*She looks horrified as John empties the bucket over Jesus*] Go and get a cloth, Timothy. John, stand in that corner and don't move!

Now, Jesus, I hope you're all right ... I'm afraid John is a little unbalanced at times ... Oh of course he's your cousin, isn't he? Well, let's hope it doesn't run in the family. Now, before we do anything else I have to fill in a registration card for you [*She picks up a card*], so if I could just have your mother's name ... [*Writes*] ... and your father's ... [*Writes; stops; looks up and stares*]

'I'VE RUN YOUR BATH FOR YOU, DAD!'

7

PARTY TIME

For children, indoors. Read Appendix 3, 'Working with Children', before using this sketch.

Characters:
　NARRATOR　played by adult
　CHILDREN'S ENTERTAINER　typically awful children's uncle, should be played by the NARRATOR
　CROWD OF GUESTS　minimum of four children
Scene:
　The scene is the courtyard of a house at Cana. At the start, only the NARRATOR is on stage. The CROWD OF GUESTS enter on cue. If there are more than four, ignore the numbering in the script and let them take it in turns to speak.

NARRATOR:
This story happened nearly 2,000 years ago at the house of Benjamin in Cana, during the most enormous party.

　　[*Party noises from offstage*]

NARRATOR:
They knew a thing or two about parties in those days—they had music ...
[CROWD *enter singing*]

NARRATOR:
They had dancing ...
[CROWD *begin dancing*]

NARRATOR:
They had good food ...
[CROWD *start miming eating*]

NARRATOR:
And they had wine!

1ST GUEST:
[*Raising imaginary glass*] Bordeaux!

2ND GUEST:
[*Raising glass*] Chablis!

3RD GUEST:
[*Raising glass*] Rheinhessen!

4TH GUEST:
[*Raising glass*] Sainsbury's!

NARRATOR:
And while the grown-ups enjoyed themselves in that quiet sophisticated way that only grown-ups can ...
[CROWD *roar and start dancing frantically*]

NARRATOR:
The children were next door having a party of their own.
[CROWD *become* CHILDREN. *They cheer and begin chasing each other in a game of tig*]

NARRATOR:
They played tig ...
[*One* CHILD *covers his eyes and begins counting while the others 'hide' onstage*]

NARRATOR:
Hide and seek ...

[*The* CHILD *who had his eyes covered turns and catches the others one by one. They start running round in a circle, singing*]

NARRATOR:

Musical chairs ...

[*They stop singing and all try to sit on imaginary chairs, ie the floor*]

NARRATOR:

And tig ...

[CHILDREN *start playing tig again*]

NARRATOR:

And hide and seek ...

[CHILDREN *play hide and seek again*]

NARRATOR:

And musical chairs ...

[CHILDREN *play musical chairs again*]

NARRATOR:

And tig ...

[CHILDREN *look a bit fed up, then start playing tig again*]

NARRATOR:

And hide and seek ...

[CHILDREN *look even more fed up, but play none the less*]

NARRATOR:

And musical chairs ...

[CHILDREN *look really fed up, some sit down, some start stomping round the imaginary chairs*]

NARRATOR:

Yes, one thing about parties in those days—they did go on a bit.

[CHILDREN *slump to the floor, exhausted*]

NARRATOR:

By the second day, they were getting really fed up.

1ST CHILD:
I've had enough of this!

2ND CHILD:
Why can't we go home?

3RD CHILD:
This is so boring!

4TH CHILD:
Even school's better than this!

NARRATOR:
So, to brighten them up, a children's entertainer was sent along ...

[The NARRATOR *becomes the* CHILDREN'S ENTERTAINER. *He does this by putting on a silly nose, or some other ridiculous prop or costume, and runs round to the front of the stage*]

ENTERTAINER:
Hi, kids, my name's Uncle Caleb. What are your names?

CHILDREN:
[*All groan*]

ENTERTAINER:
[*Mimics their groan*] Uuuuh! Well, that's a funny name ha ... ha ...

1ST CHILD:
Who is this idiot?

2ND CHILD:
I don't know.

3RD CHILD:
This party gets worse every minute.

ENTERTAINER:
[*Trying to ignore their complaints*] Now, we're going to play a game. It's called 'Hunt the Lion'. Does anybody know how to play?

[*Pause; nobody moves*]

ENTERTAINER:
Right, I'll tell you. I'm going to lead you through the

jungle, and we're all going to try and find a lion. Now, I want you all to do just what I do.

> [ENTERTAINER *faces the front, so the* CHILDREN *are behind him*]

ENTERTAINER:

Now, follow me as we go battling through the undergrowth.

> [ENTERTAINER *battles;* CHILDREN *do nothing*]

ENTERTAINER:

Oh, we've come to a swamp now, eeuch! Still, got to keep going.

> [ENTERTAINER *mimes walking through waist-deep mud.* CHILDREN *do nothing*]

ENTERTAINER:

It's getting deeper ... and deeper ... and wetter ... and wetter ... it's no use, we'll have to start swimming.

> [ENTERTAINER *mimes swimming.* CHILDREN *still do nothing*]

ENTERTAINER:

We're across the river now, and there's tall grass everywhere and ... yes, I can see lion tracks. Now we'll have to move very quietly ... sssh!

> [ENTERTAINER *creeps through the grass.* CHILDREN *look at each other and smile knowingly*]

ENTERTAINER:

Yes, there's definitely a lion nearby. Must be very, very quiet ...

> [One CHILD *counts silently. On the count of three the* CHILDREN *all roar as loudly as they can. The* ENTERTAINER *jumps with fright and turns back towards the children*]

ENTERTAINER:

Aaaah!

CHILDREN:

[*All laugh*]

ENTERTAINER:

That wasn't nice.

4TH CHILD:

But it was funny.

1ST CHILD:

Do you know any more games like that?

ENTERTAINER:

We're only going to have another game if you promise to play it properly!

2ND CHILD:

But that's boring!

3RD CHILD

I know, let's have a water fight!

CHILDREN:

[*Together*] Yes!

ENTERTAINER:

No, I don't think that's a good idea at all ...

4TH CHILD:

Where can we get some water?

1ST CHILD:

They must have some next door.

2ND CHILD:

Yeah, come on.

    [*CHILDREN all run off*]

ENTERTAINER:

What about a hopping race? That would be fun, wouldn't it? Oh dear ...

    [*ENTERTAINER removes silly nose and becomes NARRATOR again*]

NARRATOR:

Meanwhile, next door, things weren't all going to plan.

    [*CHILDREN become adult GUESTS again*]

1ST GUEST:

Run out of wine?

2ND GUEST:
We can't have run out of wine.
3RD GUEST:
We've only been here two days.
4TH GUEST:
We might as well go home if we've run out of wine.
NARRATOR:
And Jesus, who was also at the party, added to the confusion when he told the waiters to start giving people water.
1ST GUEST:
Those waiters—they're serving up water.
2ND GUEST:
They can't be!
3RD GUEST:
They are, I saw them taking it out of the water jars.
4TH GUEST:
This is a very odd party.
NARRATOR:
Just at that moment, the children came rushing in ...
    [GUESTS become CHILDREN again, and start rushing
    about looking for the water]
3RD CHILD:
So where's the water?
4TH CHILD:
In those jars over there.
    [CHILDREN run to the back of stage, and face away
    from the audience as they inspect the imaginary
    water jars]
1ST CHILD:
No, this is wine.
2ND CHILD:
But it was water yesterday.
3RD CHILD:
Well, it isn't now.

4TH CHILD:
Isn't there any other water?

NARRATOR:
But there wasn't any other water. It had all been turned into wine.

1ST CHILD:
Fancy running out of water.

2ND CHILD:
What kind of a party runs out of water?

3RD CHILD:
We'll have to do something else now.

4TH CHILD:
Yeah, but what?

    [NARRATOR *becomes* CHILDREN'S ENTERTAINER *once more and runs onstage*]

ENTERTAINER:
I know, why don't we all have a game of hunt the thimble!

CHILDREN:
[*Together, groan*]

1ST CHILD:
I've got a better idea, let's play hunt Uncle Caleb!

CHILDREN:
[*Together*] Yes!

ENTERTAINER:
No, no that's not a good idea. No!

    [CHILDREN *chase* ENTERTAINER *off the stage*]

8

INSURANCE CLAIM

From an idea by Howard Cunnington

Scene:
An office at Decapolis General Insurance. A CLAIMS
INVESTIGATOR is on the telephone. He has a form in
his hand.

CLAIMS INVESTIGATOR:
Hello, am I speaking to Benjamin of Gadara? Oh good,
my name's Philip of Decapolis from Decapolis General
Insurance. You recently lodged a claim with us for the
loss of a number of pigs, is that right? ... good. Now
your policy does cover all types of livestock, but
is conditional on you, the policyholder, taking
all reasonable steps to ensure their well-being, and
according to your claim form you lost some 2,000
head of swine in a single afternoon. Now, on the face
of it, that does sound a little bit careless ... Please,
Mr Benjamin, I'm not accusing you of anything, but
we must have a few more details before paying a claim
of this size ... of course we're not trying to wriggle out
of it, Mr Benjamin. Indeed, our company has one of
the best repayment records in the province. Did you

realise that on 75 per cent of last year's 100 per cent damage claims, we paid at least 85 per cent in all but 15 per cent of the 54 per cent of cases investigated? ... No, you didn't, did you?

Now, first, cause of death—drowning. That's a bit unusual for pigs, isn't it? Could you explain where they drowned? ... Yes, I'd rather suspected it was in the water, but which particular bit of water? ... Mr Benjamin, what were your pigs doing in the Sea of Galilee? ... They were drowning.

We don't seem to be getting very far, do we? Right, let's go one step further back, how did they get into the water in the first place? ... I see, and what prompted this stampede? ... A lunatic? What, he scared them, did he? I'm sorry, Mr Benjamin, I never realised pigs were such sensitive animals ... Who got better? ... The lunatic, well I'm delighted to hear it, but I really don't see the connection ... What 'demons', Mr Benjamin? ... The ones tormenting the madman ... [*Chuckling*] ... so these demons left the man, who enjoyed a sudden and miraculous recovery, and entered your pigs, which went completely mad, hurtled off down the hill into the Sea of Galilee and drowned ... [*Laughing*] ... well, that would explain it. And I presume you have plenty of witnesses for all this ... [*Face falls*] How many?

Mr Benjamin, let's get this absolutely straight, these animals were under supervision and behaving quite normally, until this lunatic came along, whereupon his 'demons' took a fancy to your pigs and decided to take them for a swim ... Ah! They were sent into your pigs. Tell me, who did this sending? Well you see technically he would be responsible ... [*Writing*] ... Jesus ... of ... Nazareth ... thanks. That name sound familiar, why would I have heard of him? ...

Wandering preacher. These people are a menace ...
What? Mr Benjamin, what did you just call him?
[*Smiling*] ... Oh dear, oh dear, oh dear, oh dear. I'm
afraid I have some rather bad news for you ... Well, if
you look at your policy, you'll find it states quite
clearly that it doesn't cover acts of God. Sorry [*He
hangs up*].

9

THE TREE SURGEONS

Characters:
    NATHANAEL older, fanatical about trees
    DAVID younger apprentice, more blasé
    ZACCHEUS the reformed tax-collector
Scene:
    A canteen in the Jericho Garden Maintenance
Department. There is a table with two chairs in the
centre of the room, where DAVID sits reading the
paper and eating a sandwich. To one side is another
table with tea-making facilities. NATHANAEL enters
angrily; he is carrying a sycamore branch, which he
throws to the floor.

NATHANAEL:
Look at that!
DAVID:
[*Not looking up*] Mmm?
NATHANAEL:
It's from one of the sycamores by the North Gate.
DAVID:
Mmmm.

NATHANAEL:
Vandals! They've got no respect for anything.
DAVID:
Yeah.
NATHANAEL:
Poor tree.
DAVID:
It's over there. [*He points to the tea*]
NATHANAEL:
What?
DAVID:
The tea. Isn't that what you wanted?
NATHANAEL:
I was talking about a tree.
DAVID:
What tree?
NATHANAEL:
[*Sighing*] Never mind. [*He pours himself a cup of tea*]
Your trouble is you just don't take any interest in your
work.
DAVID:
[*Sniggers at the story he is reading*]
NATHANAEL:
And don't start sniggering! I mean it. Tree surgery's
more than just a job, it's a vocation, it's a calling, it's
about getting out into the open air and facing up to the
elements, it's about learning to understand nature's
mightiest living creatures, it's about ...
DAVID:
Ha ... ha ... climbing trees!
NATHANAEL:
[*Annoyed*] No, it's not about climbing trees!
DAVID:
[*Looking up from the paper*] What? No, I meant the
man in the paper. What were you talking about?

NATHANAEL:

[*Sitting down in a huff*] No, no, don't worry about anything I say. I'm just the foreman, just the master craftsman with a lifetime's knowledge and experience to share, don't waste your time listening to me!

DAVID:

I'm interested.

NATHANAEL:

It was nothing.

DAVID:

Well, listen to this, then:

[*NATHANAEL makes a show of not paying attention*]

DAVID:

[*Reading*] 'The chief tax-collector for Jericho has been climbing trees ... '

NATHANAEL:

[*Suddenly taking an interest*] What trees?

DAVID:

One of the sycamores by the North Gate, but the point is ...

[*NATHANAEL grabs the paper from him*]

NATHANAEL:

Let me look at that!

DAVID:

But I was reading it ...

NATHANAEL:

[*Looking at paper*] So, it was him!

DAVID:

What are you talking about now?

NATHANAEL:

Zaccheus! He was the man that vandalised my sycamore tree.

DAVID:

He what?

[*NATHANAEL picks up the branch from the floor*]

NATHANAEL:
This is his doing! The vandal! The hooligan!

DAVID:
Oh come on, Nathanael, it's only a tree.

NATHANAEL:
Only a tree?

DAVID:
And it's not even ours, I mean we just look after them for the council.

NATHANAEL:
You just don't care, do you?

DAVID:
[Angrily] Look, I do my job, now can I have my paper back?

NATHANAEL:
All right!

[NATHANAEL *gives the paper back to* DAVID]

NATHANAEL:
[Huffily] So what happened?

DAVID:
When?

NATHANAEL:
In the story?

DAVID:
It's not important.

NATHANAEL:
Oh, come on!

DAVID:
Well, apparently he'd climbed the tree to get a better view of this Jesus of Nazareth ...

NATHANAEL:
Who?

DAVID:
That preacher who arrived in town the day before yesterday. The one I wanted to go and see, but you said we were too busy.

NATHANAEL:

We were!

DAVID:

I'm not arguing. Anyway, Jesus walks past all these thousands of cheering people, sees Zaccheus up the tree and says 'I'm coming round to your place for dinner.'

NATHANAEL:

[*Astonished*] He ate with him!

DAVID:

That's what it says here.

NATHANAEL:

He spent an evening with this ... this tree-mugger!

DAVID:

Zaccheus's done a lot worse than mug trees. You know, my mother went to complain about her taxes last year, so he put them up 25 per cent and billed her for his time.

NATHANAEL:

It all fits, doesn't it? Vandal, cheat. There's only one way to deal with that type, make a public example of them.

DAVID:

Well, that's what I would have said, but ...

NATHANAEL:

No 'buts', David. These people only understand one thing. Call me old-fashioned, but you have to be firm.

DAVID:

Well, it says here that after an evening with this Jesus character, he was a changed man.

NATHANAEL:

I'll believe that when I see it. I'm telling you, David, some people you can reform, but this type you just have to get off the streets ...

[*There is a knock at the door*]

DAVID:

But anyone can change.

NATHANAEL:

And my mother's an Egyptian. [NATHANAEL opens the door to admit ZACCHEUS]

ZACCHEUS:

Is this the Garden Maintenance Department?

NATHANAEL:

Yes, what can we do for you?

ZACCHEUS:

My name's Zaccheus ...

NATHANAEL:

[Threateningly] Ah!

ZACCHEUS:

I think I damaged one of your trees ... [ZACCHEUS hands a cheque to NATHANAEL] That should cover it.

NATHANAEL:

[Stunned] Ah! ... Yes.

ZACCHEUS:

Now, is David son of Zerash, here?

DAVID:

Yes.

ZACCHEUS:

I'm afraid I overcharged your mother rather badly last year. Could you give her this? [ZACCHEUS hands another cheque to DAVID]

DAVID:

[Looking at the amount] I'm sure it wasn't that much.

ZACCHEUS:

Let's say that's for inconvenience caused. Now I really must be getting along, I've got a lot more owing. Cheerio. [ZACCHEUS exits]

NATHANAEL:

    [NATHANAEL goes to the table and sits]

David, did I ever tell you about the Egyptian side of the family?

'FOR WALKING ON *WATER*?'

10

OUT OF THE WOOD

Scene:
A boat on the Sea of Galilee. THE MAST is all that can be seen, and is represented by one person standing very upright and to attention. No attempt should be made to represent the boat or any of its occupants. THE MAST can sway slightly, but apart from that does not move. If one foot is pulled back slightly there is less chance of overbalancing.

When this sketch was first performed there was an elaborate sound effect, beginning with lapping water, building up through a breeze to a full storm, and fading to water again. If you have the facilities to record this, or can choreograph a number of people to make the sounds, this is all to the good, but it is not necessary.

THE MAST:
[*Peering downwards*] Peter ... and Andrew. They must be going out to do a spot of late-night angling—good—I love it when the stars are out and ... Who's that? Maybe an apprentice ... [*More worried*] ... five,

six ... look, this hull's only insured to carry four! ...
eight, nine, how many more are there? ... Eleven,
twelve. Oh no, not another one, please not another
one ... [*Horrified*] Thirteen! Don't push off from the
shore, not with thirteen of us on board ... It's too late!
Well, I won't hold up the sail for you, I'll drop it, into
the water, and you'll all have to row back to the shore
... They're taking out the oars, they're going to row all
the way, I don't like it, not one little bit ... [*Astonished*]
And what does this one think he's doing now? He's
lying down at my feet ... He's going to sleep! Thirteen
on board and a passenger, this really is too much!

Stupid people! You think I'm just creaking, don't
you? Well I'm not just any mast you know. I'm a
cedar. I come from a very distinguished family. Some
of my branches, I'll have you know, were used to
panel the temple when it was refitted last spring. I'm
very well connected. Well, metaphorically at any
rate. Right now I'm screwed to the bottom of this hull.
Oak. Oh, I daresay it could be worse. You know, I've
seen hulls along this shoreline made of elm! Wouldn't
be seen rotting next to one of them. But even if my
hull isn't exactly acacia ... [MAST *lurches*] ... Oh, all
right, there's no need to take it personally ... Look,
don't play the innocent little sapling with me, you
lurched. Deliberately. And I'm feeling seasick. Ah,
that's what I need, a nice gentle night breeze ... quite
a strong breeze really ... more of a wind than a breeze,
in fact ... yes, definitely a wind ... [MAST *starts
swaying*] ... getting rather choppy around here, isn't
it? Extremely choppy. Might even go so far as to call it
rough ... It wasn't you lurching just then, was it? Now
stay calm, there's no need to panic, it's just a squall ...
No, it's not. All right, all right, I'm panicking! I'm
panicking! [*Looking at people in boat*] Well, it's all

very well for you people to get worried, at least you can swim for it. All I can do is wait to turn into a bit of driftwood. If I'm lucky, I'll be carved into an elephant. Why an elephant? Why do people always carve bits of driftwood into elephants? There can't be an elephant within 500 miles of here! And that's if I'm lucky. If I'm not, I'll just be a piece of firewood.

I don't believe it, the one at the bottom of the boat's still asleep ... They're waking him. He must be in charge, maybe he'll get them to try and row clear of the storm or something. Please, do something! He's getting up ... he's going to the side of the boat ... he's sticking his arms out over the side—he's going to dive in. They're abandoning ship. Don't leave me!

Oh, it's no use. I'll be firewood by morning. Some stupid peasant will have cooked her dinner over me by the end of the week!

[*Pause*]

That's odd ... I could have sworn the wind dropped just then ... The waves seem to be getting smaller ... The man at the side of the boat's sitting down again now. Did he do that? Well, just who does he think he is?

11

THE GREATEST BURGER EVER SOLD

Scene:

A room in a house where Jesus is staying. The only set that is required is a single chair for the AD-MAN to sit on.

The AD-MAN is a smartly dressed, confident salesman. He strides on to the stage and announces himself.

THE AD-MAN:

Hi! I wonder if I could talk to your Rabbi ... Mr Jesus, the very man. Good to meet you, sir. I'm Zebulun, Zebulun, son of Uriah, but call me Zeb. Everybody else does. Mind if I sit down? [*He doesn't wait for an answer and sits*] Thanks. Now I promise you this won't take long. I've had to double-park the chariot and I don't want another ticket.

Mr Jesus, I represent the Bethany Burger Company— you've probably heard the name—and we specialise in catering at large outdoor events, chariot races, religious festivals, stonings, and so on. What we generally do is set up two or three stalls selling a

variety of kosher meat products on unleavened buns,
all prepared on a genuine charcoal grill. You with me
so far? ... Right. Now I heard you in the synagogue
last week, and I don't say this lightly but I was
impressed ... no, really. I've heard them all you
know, preaching repentance, rebellion, wholefoods,
but you've got that little something that sets you apart
from the rest, and I can see you being one of the big
names in the years to come. Now I'm not saying you're
going to be another Nimrod of Arimathea, but who
knows? ... [*He raises his eyes*] Yes, I suppose he does,
doesn't he. But one way or another, Mr Jesus, you are
going to have an awful lot of people coming out to see
you, and that's where we come in.

Now I hear you've got a big sermon coming up on a
mount not far from here, and I thought this might be a
good opportunity for you to try us out ... 'Man shall
not live by bread alone'. That's good, that's very good,
we'll write that above the stalls if you like: 'Man shall
not live by bread alone, but by a Bethany Burger
between two slices' ... You don't like it, do you? ...
No, I could tell from that little sigh you're not happy.
OK, how about a plain 'Bethany Burgers, as recom-
mended by Jesus of Nazareth—the people's prophet'?
You've never tried one? No problem, we'll send you
one in the post. There's no hurry, these things keep for
months without gaining any flavour. Just have a taste
between now and the appointed time, that'll be enough
for the advertising standards people ... You're still
not happy are you? OK, no signs, just a couple of
stalls, and so long as you could mention the company
name a couple of times during the sermon, that'd be
great. For instance, off the top of my head: 'Blessed are
the Bethany Burger Company, for they bring nourish-
ment', or perhaps: 'Come to me you who are heavy

laden, and I'll get you a Bethany Burger with extra relish'? ...

With all due respect, Mr Jesus, you're not being very constructive. I mean, it's not as if we're asking you to do this for nothing ... It's not cashing in! It's sensible business practice. I mean, look at what goes on in the temple, but you wouldn't accuse the High Priest of 'cashing in', would you? ... You would. And just what do you intend to do about that, Mr Jesus? Drive out the moneychangers singlehandedly? It's the way the world works, you and I aren't going to change that.

We want to help you Mr Jesus. Just suppose you get three, four, five thousand guys turning out to hear this sermon of yours, they bring their families, they bring their kids. What are you going to do when they get hungry? ... [*Nodding slowly*] Uhu. I see.

[*He stands*] It's been good talking to you, sir. We'll be in touch. [*He leaves*]

'WHAT DO YOU MEAN, YOU
DON'T LIKE FISH??''

12

IN THE CANTEEN

Characters:
ANN manageress of a mobile sandwich bar, an experienced caterer
LYDIA her assistant, new to the job
Scene:
A small sandwich tent. Jesus is outside, preaching. There are cups, saucers and sandwiches laid out on a table. ANN is relaxed, reading a magazine. LYDIA is tense, peering out the door of the tent.

LYDIA:
He isn't half going on.
ANN:
[*Not looking up*] The longer he talks, the hungrier they get, the hungrier they get ...
LYDIA: } [*Together*] The more they pay ...
ANN:
LYDIA:
I know, I know. I just don't like all this hanging about.

ANN:
Make the most of it. You won't know what's hit you when the rush starts.

LYDIA:
[Giggles]

ANN:
What is it?

LYDIA:
He's just said if somebody hits you, you shouldn't hit him back.

ANN:
What does he say you should do?

LYDIA:
[Straining to hear. Looks puzzled] Give him a bit of cheek.

ANN:
He'd just hit you again if you did that.
    [Pause]

LYDIA:
You done many of these wandering preachers then?

ANN:
[Putting down the magazine] Oh, I done them all.

LYDIA:
Who was your favourite?

ANN:
Difficult to say, but I always had a soft spot for that John the Baptist.

LYDIA:
You never did, John the Baptist!

ANN:
I did! Well, just think about it. All those people wandering out into the wilderness getting dunked in the Jordan and told to repent. I mean, you'd need a cup of tea after that.

LYDIA:

I suppose so.

ANN:

Got fed up making locust and honey sandwiches, though.

LYDIA:

Done this one before?

ANN:

Jesus of Nazareth? No, he's new.

LYDIA:

[*Peering out of the door*] He's ever so popular.

ANN:

All the better for us.

LYDIA:

But there must be thousands of them, we've never got enough to go round.

ANN:

So the prices go up.

LYDIA:

They won't like that.

ANN:

Then they'll have to lump it. It's just a question of supply and demand.

LYDIA:

You don't think they'll start fighting, do you?

ANN:

No.

LYDIA:

You sure?

ANN:

I'm sure.

LYDIA:

Really sure?

ANN:

Really sure.

LYDIA:

Absolutely, completely and utterly sure?

ANN:

Yes!

[*Pause*]

LYDIA:

How can you be so certain?

ANN:

Because they never fight at these big sermons.

LYDIA:

You mean, you never get any trouble?

ANN:

Well, I wouldn't say that. I mean they don't fight with each other, that's true, but they can be ever so awkward.

LYDIA:

How do you mean?

ANN:

Well, I remember this one bloke who told folk that all that really mattered was eating the right things.

LYDIA:

What's wrong with that?

ANN:

I used to get hundreds of people asking for yoghurt and fruit juice.

LYDIA:

[*Looking out of the door*] Would you believe it?

ANN:

What is it now?

LYDIA:

He's just pinched some little kid's packed lunch.

ANN:

What's he doing with it?

LYDIA:

[*Peering into the distance*] He's got a fish in one hand,

a loaf in the other, and he's looking up at the sky talking to himself.

ANN:

They're a funny lot, these preachers.

LYDIA:

Ah! They're moving.

ANN:

Right, Lydia, this is it. Man the teapots!

> [*LYDIA and ANN take up positions, ready to serve tea. There is a pause*]

LYDIA:

When's the rush?

ANN:

Any minute.

LYDIA:

Any minute?

ANN:

Just you wait.

> [*Pause*]

LYDIA:

I'm waiting.

ANN:

[*Irritably*] All right Lydia!

> [*Pause. ANN sidles over to the door and peers out*]

ANN:

I thought you said they were moving.

LYDIA:

They were.

ANN:

Well they're not now.

> [*LYDIA moves over to the door and peers out*]

LYDIA:

But they weren't sitting like that before.

ANN:

How many different ways can you sit?

LYDIA:

Well, now they're sitting in little groups, see?

[ANN *goes back to her seat and picks up her
magazine*]

ANN:

Look, just tell me when they're coming, OK?

LYDIA:

[*Defensively*] OK.

[*Pause*]

LYDIA:

[*Staring out of the door, incredulous*] Ann!

ANN:

[*Wearily*] What is it now, Lydia?

LYDIA:

I think you should come and have a look.

ANN:

I don't.

LYDIA:

They're all eating, Ann.

ANN:

What? Grass? Each other?

LYDIA:

No, fish.

ANN:

Don't be silly, Lydia.

LYDIA:

They are!

ANN:

Lydia, where do fish come from?

LYDIA:

What are you talking about?

ANN:

They come from the sea, don't they? Do you know
how far it is to the sea from here?

LYDIA:
They've got bread as well.

ANN:
So they've been to the baker's too. My goodness, they must have been moving fast when you saw them.

LYDIA:
Well, come and have a look.

[ANN *reluctantly puts down her magazine and goes to the door. She looks out*]

ANN:
Lydia.

LYDIA:
Ann?

ANN:
They're all eating.

LYDIA:
But all they had was that one kid's lunch.

ANN:
What was it?

LYDIA:
Five or six rolls. And a couple of fish.

ANN:
Five rolls, and two fish, between 5,000. We've got 400 sandwiches and sixteen gallons of tea between the two of us.

[*Long pause*]

LYDIA:
Fancy a cuppa?

13

ALL IN THE MIND

Characters:
  WILL POWER decisive, in charge
  MORALITY thoughtful, anxious
  SELF-INTEREST carefree, 'bit of a lad'
Scene:
  Inside somebody's brain. There are three desks facing the audience. The central 'command' desk belongs to WILL POWER; MORALITY is slightly further back and on the right; SELF-INTEREST is similarly positioned on the left. Initially, the desks are all empty; WILL POWER enters first and goes to his.

WILL POWER:
[*Speaking into imaginary intercom*] Central Nervous System, Central Nervous System, this is brain, Will Power speaking, we are about to get out of bed, repeat, we are about to get out of bed, eyes open, arms stretch, legs standby ...
MORALITY:
[*Enters yawning*] Morning, Will!

WILL POWER:

Legs swing, body raise, feet to the floor and stand! Now let's have another yawn and a stretch. [*Turning to* MORALITY] Morning, Morality, how are you?

MORALITY:

A bit low on fibre.

WILL POWER:

Where's Self-Interest?

MORALITY:

Haven't seen him.

WILL POWER:

Tut! Late again. [*To intercom again*] OK, body, go for clothes, go for clothes, they're at the far side of the bedroom.

[SELF-INTEREST *enters in dressing-gown*]

SELF-INTEREST:

[*Yawning*] Morning!

WILL POWER:

You're late!

SELF-INTEREST:

I know.

WILL POWER:

That's the third time this week.

SELF-INTEREST:

Yeah ... yeah ...

[*They all lurch as if the whole room has suddenly had a great jolt.* MORALITY *and* WILL POWER, *who are seated at their respective desks, bump into the air, and* SELF-INTEREST, *who up until now has been standing, falls across his desk*]

SELF-INTEREST:

What was that?

WILL POWER:

[*Irritated*] We just tripped. [*To intercom*] Damage report. [*Turning to* SELF-INTEREST] This is your fault!

SELF-INTEREST:
My fault!
WILL POWER:
Physical well-being is your responsibility. Now get to work.

[*SELF-INTEREST sits and begins working*]

MORALITY:
We've got some rather bad language going on at the moment.
WILL POWER:
[*To intercom*] Voice, tone it down a bit. [*Reading something*] No serious damage done. [*To intercom*] OK, body, we're getting dressed, switching to auto-pilot. [*Flicks a switch*]
SELF-INTEREST:
Why the rush?
WILL POWER:
Because we've got an important meeting in ... [*Looking up at imaginary clock in front of him*] ... three minutes. [*To MORALITY*] Oh, Memory was jogging this morning, he left this:

[*WILL POWER hands MORALITY a memo*]

MORALITY:
[*Reading*] Oh, it's Mother's birthday.
SELF-INTEREST:
So what?
MORALITY:
We need to get a present.
SELF-INTEREST:
Why?
MORALITY:
Well, because she'd appreciate it.
SELF-INTEREST:
You always want to spend money on other people.

MORALITY:
We can afford it.
SELF-INTEREST:
Not for much longer the way you're going.
MORALITY:
Look, we're rich.
SELF-INTEREST:
Only compared to people like your mother.
MORALITY:
Oh, stop rationalising!
SELF-INTEREST:
Don't tell me my job!
WILL POWER:
No time now, we'll go on the way back. OK, dressing completed, we're going back to manual. [*To intercom*] Out the door, turn left and head for the temple.
SELF-INTEREST:
Who is it we're going to see?
WILL POWER:
Jesus.
SELF-INTEREST:
Who?
MORALITY:
He's a very important teacher ...
SELF-INTEREST:
Oh no, not more commandments!
WILL POWER:
Beggar ahead!
MORALITY:
Give him some money.
SELF-INTEREST:
Tell him to find a job.
WILL POWER:
Let's settle for a patronising smile, shall we? [*To intercom*] You get that face?

SELF-INTEREST:

What do you want to hear another teacher for?

MORALITY:

This one's different from the others.

SELF-INTEREST:

Oh, I don't doubt it. What's his speciality? Proper footwear for religious festivals? Fingernail polishing for Pharisees?

MORALITY:

Don't be silly!

SELF-INTEREST:

You tell me not to be silly! You're the one that spends twenty minutes checking your files every time anybody offers us a sandwich. No wonder we don't get invited to dinner parties any more.

WILL POWER:

Hundred yards to temple, Jesus of Nazareth coming into view.

SELF-INTEREST:

So what does he talk about?

MORALITY:

Life.

SELF-INTEREST:

[*Sarcastically*] So we can make sure we're alive. Well, I suppose it'll be good to hear it from an expert.

MORALITY:

No! We've got important things to discuss.

SELF-INTEREST:

So what are you going to say to him?

MORALITY:

Well, I thought we'd start with something respectful like, um, 'Good teacher ...' [*Tails off*]

SELF-INTEREST:

You've dragged us all the way down here so you can tell him he's a good teacher?

WILL POWER:
Twenty-five yards to temple, Jesus has seen us. [*To intercom*] Voice, stand by. First question, Morality?

MORALITY:
Yes, 'Good teacher ...'

SELF-INTEREST:
Ask him how we get to live for ever.

WILL POWER:
[*To intercom*] You get that voice? The question is 'Good teacher, how can I live for ever?'

MORALITY:
That's stupid!

SELF-INTEREST:
Not as stupid as saying nothing.

WILL POWER:
[*Reading off an imaginary screen in front of him*] And the answer's coming through. He wants to know why we called him good. [*To* SELF-INTEREST] Well?

SELF-INTEREST:
[*Pointing at* MORALITY] His idea.

MORALITY:
Yes ... um ... well ...

WILL POWER:
[*To intercom*] OK, we're playing for time, face frown, right hand, scratch head ... Oh it's all right, he's talking again. [*Reading*] He's asking us if we know the commandments.

MORALITY:
Just the usual ones?

WILL POWER:
Yeah.

SELF-INTEREST:
[*To* MORALITY] I told you this was a waste of time.

WILL POWER:
[*To intercom*] We've done those.

SELF-INTEREST:
We should have stayed in bed.
MORALITY:
Oh shut up!
WILL POWER:
[*Reading*] He says we've missed out one thing ...
MORALITY:
Ha! Told you he'd have something new to say.
SELF-INTEREST:
Tut, more rules.
MORALITY:
Worth it, though.
SELF-INTEREST:
Perhaps.
MORALITY:
Oh, don't be short-sighted, Self-Interest, of course it is.
WILL POWER:
[*Staring in front of him*] You're not going to like it.
MORALITY:
Come on, it can't be that bad.
WILL POWER:
Yes, it can.
SELF-INTEREST:
Well, what is it?
WILL POWER:
We've got to sell everything ...
SELF-INTEREST:
What?
WILL POWER:
And give the money away.
    [*SELF-INTEREST strides over to* WILL POWER's *desk*]
MORALITY:
Oh dear.

SELF-INTEREST:
[*Looking at* 'screen'] The man's mad.

WILL POWER:
So what do we do?

SELF-INTEREST:
Leave. He's off his head.

MORALITY:
I think that's rather harsh.

SELF-INTEREST:
So what do you think he is?

MORALITY:
He's a great teacher ...

SELF-INTEREST:
He's a loony!

MORALITY:
There might be something in what he says.

SELF-INTEREST:
[*To* MORALITY] Look! This isn't just something else to add to your list.

WILL POWER:
He's right, Morals. This affects all of us.

MORALITY:
What if he's right?

SELF-INTEREST:
Right about what?

MORALITY:
About living for ever.

SELF-INTEREST:
[*Laughing*] Oh come on, you don't believe that, do you?

MORALITY:
Um ... well ...

WILL POWER:
He's still waiting for an answer.

SELF-INTEREST:
Let's go.

WILL POWER:
[*To intercom*] OK, legs, we're leaving ...
SELF-INTEREST:
[*Muttering*] I knew it was a waste of time.
WILL POWER:
[*Reading off screen*] Stomach's grumbling. Says he's still waiting for breakfast.
SELF-INTEREST:
Right, what do you say to a bacon sandwich?
MORALITY:
I've told you before, we don't eat pork!
WILL POWER:
[*Sighing*] Here we go again.

14

THE FUNERAL

Scene:
MRS LAZARUS' front room. MRS LAZARUS is dressed in black and has a black handbag on her lap. She is relating the story of her husband's funeral to a number of her friends.

MRS LAZARUS:
You know, I don't know whether I've been coming or going these last few days, what with all the arrangements for the funeral, the food, the mourners, the invitations—half of them never replied, you know ... No. It really makes you wonder if folk have a shred of decency left when they can't be bothered answering a funeral invitation. Oh, I gave them the benefit of the doubt, and presumed they'd all died or something, but no, there they all were on the day to pay their last respects to my Lazarus. And eat my vol-au-vents.

Lazarus always used to say how much he enjoyed my vol-au-vents, always did. Come to think of it, he never used to say very much else. Still, mustn't speak ill of the dead, and he was always nice to me. About my vol-au-vents, although I must say I hadn't expected him to be eating them on this particular occasion, what with it being his funeral and all, but I could hardly refuse when he asked, well could I? ... No.

I mean, it had all been going so nicely up until then. The food was nice, the drink was nice, the mourners were nice, it was all very nice, until this Jesus of Nazareth turned up—late—and all his disciples. They seemed a bit scruffy to me, carpenters, fishermen— you know the type—but he had been very friendly with my Lazurus so I asked him in and offered him a vol-au-vent. You know, he paid no attention. He was too busy. Weeping ... Aye. Well, he could have had his vol-au-vent first and wept after, but no, no, he just wept straight off, and there was worse to come, because no sooner had he finished weeping than he told those men of his to start opening up the tomb.

Honestly, these provincial types are all the same, no sense of propriety. I mean, I don't suppose it ever occurred to him to ask me if it was all right. I'd just spent three days with practically no sleep, writing invitations and making vol-au-vents, when in strolls this wandering monk with his gang of ... artisans, and starts disrupting the whole occasion.

Well, I wasn't going to let my own husband's funeral turn into some kind of tradesmen's jamboree, so I went over to this Jesus and told him—politely but firmly—to behave himself or leave. He paid no attention, as I might have expected, and started calling out Lazarus' name. 'Lazarus,' he said, 'come out!' 'It won't do any good,' I told him, 'he's dead.' And he was. 'No I'm not,' said Lazarus. Would you believe it! While I'd been stood there talking, he'd come out of his tomb and sneaked up behind me. Well, I was quite taken aback. It was all I could do to offer him a vol-au-vent.

He took it. He took quite a few. Dying had obviously taken a lot out of him.

Well, once we'd all got over the initial shock, everybody else had a great time, and Lazarus—I don't think I've ever seen anyone enjoy his own funeral so much. Personally, I felt quite embarrassed. There I was trying to run a decent funeral when the dearly departed turns up as the star guest—I mean, it was lovely to see him and all, but it really was quite inconvenient. And now, you see, I don't know what to do, because officially I'm still in mourning. We all are. Apart from Lazarus, so he really got the best deal all round.

Still, at least the vol-au-vents got eaten. Lazarus did say how much he enjoyed my vol-au-vents. Everybody loved my vol-au-vents.

[MRS LAZARUS *opens her bag, takes out a vol-au-vent, and pops it into her mouth*]

You know, I think I might try prawn next time.

'LAZARUS! HOW'VE YOU BEEN?!'

15

THE PHARISEE RAP

Explanation:
Although this is written in the character of a Pharisee, it is more important to go for rhythm and style than characterisation. There are four beats per line, apart from the very last one. If you are in any doubt about how to deliver a rap, which is somewhere between speaking and singing, have a listen to Run DMC, or some other rapping band.

A well-delivered rap is very compelling, and will work equally well indoors or in the open air.

PHARISEE:
I am a Pharisee, how do you do,
I'm a real big wheel in the temple crew,
So listen hard to what I'm saying to you,
And do just what I tell you to.

I say sit straight, don't stare,
Clean those shoes and brush that hair,
Shout 'Hallelujah!', say a short prayer,
And throw those arms into the air.

If you wanna be religious then you gotta be smart,
You gotta do it all like it's from the heart,
You gotta look good—it's quite an art,
But don't ever forget, you're just playing a part.

I say snap [*Snap fingers*], clap [*Clap hands*], put on
   your hat,
What you really are doesn't matter a scrap,
So long as you look good you don't need to flap,
And then we can all do the Pharisee rap!

Now I know there's a man with a different song,
He's a carpenter and he says I'm wrong,
Well, he's too hot-headed and he's too headstrong,
And I'm telling you now that he won't last long.

I met him only yesterday,
As I was going to the temple for a public pray,
That man, he stood right in my way,
And I couldn't believe what I heard him say.

He said 'Hey you! Pharisee!
So proud of all your piety,
You lead, and yet you cannot see,
Your business is hypocrisy.

'I speak the truth, be in no doubt,
It isn't enough just to act devout,
You have to change from the inside out,
Your moral code is up the spout!'

Well, I confess, I could not see
How such a thing as this could be,
That a friend of sinners should disagree
With a man as good and pure as me.

So I said, 'You say I'm not upright,
And yet I always do what's right,
And I do it all in public sight,
But you just want to pick a fight!

'I keep the laws I pay my dues,
I see my religious duties through,
I eat what's right, and unlike you,
I make sure all my friends do too.'

He said, 'You give me platitudes
About good manners and good food,
But the selfish pride that you exude
Is a far worse sin than being rude.

'Don't you know there should be a link
Between the things you say and you think?
I don't care what you eat and drink,
But pious words without action stink.'

Well, every single word he spoke
Was clearly said just to provoke,
This thing had gone beyond a joke,
I simply had to go for broke.

I said 'This man, who is he?
What is his authority?
His training is in carpentry,
But I am a qualified Pharisee!'

He said, 'It's no use pulling rank,
'Cos we're not fooled by all your swank,
Now for once in all your life be frank,
And admit your argument just sank.'

Well, the crowd went wild, and with a cry,
They lifted him up, shoulder high,
And I could only watch and sigh,
As they turned to me and said 'Nice try'.

Well, as the people carried him away,
I guess he thought he'd won the day,
But I guarantee that come what may,
One day soon I'm going to make him pay.

I'm going after the man from Nazareth,
I'm going to hunt him down till my dying breath,
I'm going to hound him to an early death,
I'm going to get you—Jesus of Nazareth.

I say snap [*Snap fingers*], clap [*Clap hands*], put on
    your hat,
What you really are doesn't matter a scrap,
So long as you look good, you don't need to flap,
And then we can all do the Pharisee, Pharisee, Pharisee,
Pharisee rap!

16

THE GARDEN

Characters:
PETER
JOHN

Scene:
The Garden of Gethsemane just before Jesus is arrested. It is cold. PETER is sitting upright but has fallen asleep. JOHN's head is slowly sinking on to his chest, but he sits up sharply, trying to stay awake. He sees PETER sleeping and tries to wake him.

JOHN:
Peter ...
PETER:
[*Half asleep*] Mmm?
JOHN:
Peter, wake up!
PETER:
What? ... Oh no, how long was I asleep?
JOHN:
A few minutes.

PETER:
Where's Jesus?

JOHN:
Where he's been all night.

PETER:
Still praying?

JOHN:
I think so.

PETER:
What about?

JOHN:
Can't tell, he's too far away.

PETER:
[*Trying to make himself more comfortable*] How much
longer are we supposed to sit here?

JOHN:
I don't know.

PETER:
'Wait here', that's all he said. Wait for what?

JOHN:
[*Snapping irritably*] Peter, I don't know!

PETER:
All right, all right, I was only asking. It's so cold.
    [*Pause*]

JOHN:
He looks terrible.

PETER:
He's probably freezing, too.

JOHN:
It's almost as if he was ... scared.

PETER:
Oh, don't be ridiculous!

JOHN:
I'm not being ridiculous, Peter. Look at him!

PETER:

[*Trying to convince himself*] He can't be scared, John, he's got power—power over evil, power over sickness, power over death itself—what could he be scared of?

JOHN:

I don't know. Look at him sweating, something's wrong, Peter.

PETER:

Maybe we should get a doctor ...

JOHN:

I thought he had power over sickness.

PETER:

Well, yes but ... yes.

JOHN:

Anyway, we can't afford one till Judas gets back. What's going on?

PETER:

I don't know ... just so tired ... [*His head sinks on to his chest*]

JOHN:

What was he talking about tonight?

PETER:

[*Half asleep*] Mmm?

JOHN:

[*Shaking* PETER] Peter, Peter, wake up!

PETER:

[*Waking again*] Sorry.

JOHN:

For weeks he's been talking about Jerusalem as if there was ... nothing beyond ...

PETER:

What do you mean?

JOHN:

Well, all those things he said tonight about his blood. It's almost as if ...

PETER:

No, he's not going to die. That's what you're thinking, aren't you? But the Messiah can't die, the Son of God can't die!

JOHN:

So what's going to happen?

PETER:

Nothing's going to happen.

JOHN:

What do you mean nothing? Do you mean we're all going to carry on travelling round Judea till we retire?

PETER:

I don't worry about the future.

JOHN:

You can't get out of it that easily, Peter. You've said he's the Messiah, well, what do you think the Messiah's going to do? Rebuild Israel? Throw out the Romans? Conquer the world?

PETER:

I don't know, John! I used to think I knew, but not any more.

JOHN:

And what are we doing up here?

PETER:

I don't know.

JOHN:

Look at him, Peter, he's in pain.

PETER:

Perhaps that's why he wanted to get away from the city.

JOHN:

But it doesn't make any sense. First, he enters Jerusalem on a colt, then he throws the moneychangers out of the temple. Can you think of two things more guaranteed to upset the authorities?

PETER:

No ...

JOHN:

So you'd expect him to stay among the crowds, among his supporters, but no, ever since, we've been skulking around in private rooms and lonely hill-sides. I could almost believe he was setting himself up ...

PETER:

Stop it! I know what you're going to say and you're wrong. Nobody is going to lay a finger on him.

JOHN:

I thought you didn't know what was going to happen.

PETER:

I don't. But I do know that nothing can happen to him if he doesn't want it to happen.

JOHN:

Don't you understand? That's what I'm afraid of ...

PETER:

[*Dozing off*] Mmm?

JOHN:

What if he wants to be caught?

    [PETER *says nothing;* JOHN *starts to doze as well. They both wake with a jump*]

PETER:

What's that noise?

JOHN:

What? ... Only Judas. [*He looks to where Judas is coming from*] Who are those people with him?

17

THE MOBSTERS

Suitable for street-theatre.

Characters:

THE BOSS (Caiaphas) quiet, ruthless, Al Capone-style gang leader

1ST HEAVY (Annas) his second-in-command

2ND HEAVY a thug

JUDAS the squealer

PILATE the harassed police chief under pressure from the mob

JESUS

Scene:

THE BOSS' headquarters in Jerusalem. Will later become PILATE's residence. No set is required.

Initially, the cast are offstage providing the sound of distant cheering. THE BOSS enters. The 1ST HEAVY enters a few seconds later.

BOSS:
What's that noise?

1ST HEAVY:
They're welcoming him, Boss.

BOSS:
Welcoming who?
1ST HEAVY:
The carpenter.
BOSS:
What's he doing?
1ST HEAVY:
Just lapping it up.
BOSS:
He's got no right!
1ST HEAVY:
They're saying he's the king.
BOSS:
We got to watch him, Annas, he's out of control.
   [2ND HEAVY runs in]
2ND HEAVY:
He just hit the temple, Boss!
BOSS:
He what!
2ND HEAVY:
He turned over the tables and threw out the traders.
BOSS:
He's gone too far.
1ST HEAVY:
Do we hit him, Boss?
BOSS:
No, he's got too big for that now. This thing's got to be
done legit.
   [BOSS looks at 2ND HEAVY, snaps his fingers and
   points to the door. 2ND HEAVY exits]
1ST HEAVY:
So what do we do, Boss?
BOSS:
We wait. He's finished, and he knows it.

[2ND HEAVY *returns holding* JUDAS *by the collar. He throws* JUDAS *to the floor*]

2ND HEAVY:

Here's the squealer, Boss. Name's Judas.

BOSS:

What can you do for us, Judas?

JUDAS:

I can get you the carpenter.

BOSS:

So get him for me.

JUDAS:

Hey! I'm not sticking my neck out for nothing.

BOSS:

How much?

JUDAS:

Thirty pieces.

BOSS:

[*To* 1ST HEAVY] Pay him the money.

[1ST HEAVY *throws a bag of money to the floor.* JUDAS *picks it up*]

BOSS:

Where?

JUDAS:

Gethsemane.

BOSS:

When?

JUDAS:

Tonight.

BOSS:

How will we know him?

JUDAS:

I'll be with him. Is that OK?

BOSS:

OK. Now get him out of here!

[2ND HEAVY *drags* JUDAS *out*]

1ST HEAVY:
What's the plan, Boss?
BOSS:
First, we pick up the carpenter. Then we pay a little social call to our tame governor. It's a long time since I spoke to Pilate.

> [BOSS *and* 1ST HEAVY *exit,* PILATE *enters from the opposite side and starts pacing back and forth across the stage. The* BOSS, 1ST HEAVY *and* 2ND HEAVY *dragging* JESUS *enter as* PILATE *is pacing away from them.* 2ND HEAVY *throws* JESUS *to the floor.* PILATE *turns to face them*]

2ND HEAVY:
Get up!

> [2ND HEAVY *roughly pulls* JESUS *to his feet*]

BOSS:
Good to see you, Pilate.
PILATE:
[*Not pleased to see the* BOSS] I wish I could say the same, Caiaphas.
BOSS:
Oh, now what's wrong? I haven't upset you, have I?
PILATE:
Oh no, no, it's two o'clock on a Thursday morning; you're just the guy I wanted to see. Now what do you want?
BOSS:
Just a friendly chat.
PILATE:
[*Sarcastically*] Oh, terrific! Say, it's been kind of warm lately, don't you think? Now say what you want and get out!
BOSS:
OK, Pilate. If that's the way you want it. [*Pointing to* JESUS] I want him.

PILATE:
So, you've got him.
BOSS:
You don't understand, Pilate. I want him dead.
> [BOSS *snaps his fingers.* 1ST HEAVY *hands him a
> piece of paper.* BOSS *offers it to* PILATE]
BOSS:
Here's the warrant. Sign it. Please.
PILATE:
[*Pushing the warrant aside*] So what's he done?
BOSS:
He's been making some threats.
PILATE:
And you want him dead for that?
BOSS:
He's been upsetting a lot of people.
PILATE:
Upsetting people isn't a crime, Caiaphas.
BOSS:
He's dangerous, Pilate!
PILATE:
To whom, Caiaphas?
BOSS:
To all of us. That man over there is a revolutionary.
How do you think old Emperor Tiberius would like it
if you found yourself with a rebellion on your hands
in six months' time?
PILATE:
He doesn't like me much, anyway.
BOSS:
He'd like you a whole lot less.
PILATE:
Give me the warrant.
> [BOSS *hands* PILATE *the warrant*]

PILATE:

[Signing it] I take no responsibility for this.

    [PILATE hands the warrant back to the BOSS]

Now get out.

    [All exit. The cast make the sound of jeering and abuse directed at Jesus on the cross. The BOSS and the 1ST HEAVY enter]

BOSS:

I hate crucifixions. They're messy.

1ST HEAVY:

Do you think it was really necessary, Boss?

BOSS:

It was him or us, Annas. It was him or us.

[They leave]

18

THE CENTURION

Scene:
A room somewhere in Jerusalem two weeks after the crucifixion. The CENTURION who had been in charge is relating what happened. He is tense, and smoking a cigarette.

CENTURION:

I was on duty last Friday, in charge of crucifixions ... Oh, I volunteered for it—you see it entitled me to extra leave. And anyway, I'd done it before ... in fact, I'm really quite an expert. For instance, did you know that there are two distinct types of crucifixion? ... There's ropes, and there's nails. With ropes, you tie them up there and they take two, maybe three days to die of thirst, or exposure. With nails, it's a bit quicker and a lot messier. Friday was a nails job.

And there's another thing people get wrong—you see, most folk think the nails go in here, [*Demonstrate*] through the palms of the hands. Well of course if we did that, the flesh would tear, and he'd fall off the cross the moment we stood him up. No, in fact, they go in just here, [*Demonstrate*] above the wrist, between the two bones of the forearm, and you've got to be careful you don't hit that artery, or he'd die in ten minutes. Of course it's round about there that all the nerves come into the hand.

You know it's always amazed me how long they can stay alive up there. What with the flogging and dragging the cross up the hill themselves, they usually look half dead by the time they get there, and it's hard work hanging from a cross, 'cos, you see, when you're hanging from your arms stretched out like this, [*Demonstrate*] you can't breathe. Every time you want to take a breath, you have to push up on the nail through your feet. So it alternates, see, one minute you're choking to death, and the next you can't think for the pain.

Still, there's crucifixion for you, and it's never bothered me ... until last Friday. There was a carpenter, 'a subversive' they said, 'a dangerous man'. There was supposed to be something funny about his trial, I don't know about that, but there was something funny about his execution all right.

When we lay him out on the ground to put the nails in, he just accepted it. Well, usually they kick and scream and shout and throw every curse they can think of ... well, understandably. But he just lay there. I thought perhaps he was unconscious, so I shouted something at him—I can't remember what—and he turned towards me. I had to look away. I felt naked, helpless. I was scared. I was scared of a condemned carpenter.

When we got the crossbar into position, I heard him speak for the first time. I couldn't believe it. I didn't want to believe it, but you know, I could have sworn he was forgiving us. Why? Why couldn't he just curse us and be done with it? I could have understood that. I felt sick. I wanted to run away, but I was on duty till sunset, so I stood, shaking, with my back to the cross.

Next thing was, about midday it must have been, the sky went dark. By that time I was in a cold sweat, but I wasn't going to run! But it was dark, really dark. No thunder, no lightning, nothing spectacular, just darkness. Like the middle of the night.

Then, about half-way through the afternoon, the earth began to shake, and I heard the carpenter shouting above the noise: 'It's finished!' I didn't know what I was doing or what I was saying, I fell on my knees, I called out, 'He really was the Son of God!'

The sky cleared. I looked up. I saw the carpenter. He was dead.

And now they're saying he's risen, his followers. You know, I almost wish it was true, but if it is—even if it isn't—who was he? Who have I killed? Did he forgive me? I don't know. [Pause. *He grinds out the cigarette*] I don't know.

'TAKE THAT TO THE FORENSIC
LAB AT TURIN.'

19

THE CASE OF THE MISSING CORPSE

Suitable for street-theatre.

Characters:
> HOLMES   the great detective, a bit louder than the original
> WATSON   his assistant

Scene:
> The garden outside the tomb where Jesus was buried. HOLMES is on stage, thinking. He is wearing a false nose and moustache. WATSON runs in.

WATSON:
Holmes! Holmes!

HOLMES:
[Turning *towards* WATSON] Yes!

WATSON:
But ... who are you?

> [*HOLMES removes his disguise*]

HOLMES:
Don't worry, Watson, it's only me.

WATSON:
You startled me. Holmes, a mystery is afoot.

HOLMES:
On the contrary, Watson, I understand my feet
perfectly.

WATSON:
But a crime has been committed!

HOLMES:
And were feet involved?

WATSON:
Very likely.

HOLMES:
Tell me your tale.

WATSON:
Earlier today, a group of Roman soldiers ...

HOLMES:
Wait! Did you say Roman soldiers?

WATSON:
I did.

HOLMES:
I see.

WATSON:
The soldiers were guarding a tomb outside Jerusalem ...

HOLMES:
Jerusalem!

WATSON:
Yes.

HOLMES:
Continue.

WATSON:
The soldiers were guarding the tomb, but somehow
they all fell asleep at the same time, and when they
awoke, the body had gone.

HOLMES:
Watson?

WATSON:
Holmes?

HOLMES:
I am afraid I have some rather disturbing news. This is no ordinary mystery, because it is taking place in Israel, about the year 33 AD!

WATSON:
Are you certain?

HOLMES:
Consider the facts, Watson. Is there any other rational explanation?

WATSON:
Of course, that would explain the heat ...

HOLMES:
Of course.

WATSON:
And the dust.

HOLMES:
Naturally.

WATSON:
And the fact that the fellow who told me this wore a toga and spoke Latin!

HOLMES:
Precisely!

WATSON:
But Holmes?

HOLMES:
Watson?

WATSON:
How did we get here?

HOLMES:
Elementary, my dear Watson. Dramatic licence. Now, show me to the tomb where the body was laid.

>   [*HOLMES and WATSON take two or three short steps across the stage*]

HOLMES:
So, this is the tomb where the body was laid.
WATSON:
The very same.
HOLMES:
And it was sealed.
WATSON:
Naturally.
HOLMES:
And guarded.
WATSON:
Indeed.
HOLMES:
So, a dead body escapes from a sealed tomb.
WATSON:
A mystery indeed, Holmes.
HOLMES:
And yet there is a simple explanation.
WATSON:
There is?
HOLMES:
That body was not dead!
WATSON:
What?
HOLMES:
I shall demonstrate. [*He gestures towards an imaginary rock*] This 'pebble' was used to seal the tomb, was it not?
WATSON:
I believe so.
HOLMES:
Well, the body simply awoke, pushed aside the stone ... [*HOLMES attempts to push aside the imaginary rock, but is unable to do so*] Give me a hand, Watson.

[HOLMES *and* WATSON *both push desperately hard, but are unable to move the rock*]

HOLMES:
Well, he was a carpenter, wasn't he? Sturdy chap like that wouldn't have had a problem.

WATSON:
Even after being flogged?

HOLMES:
No trouble.

WATSON:
And nailed to a cross?

HOLMES:
Not in principle ...

WATSON:
And speared?

HOLMES:
Well ...

WATSON:
And sealed in a tomb without food or water for forty-eight hours?

HOLMES:
My point exactly!

WATSON:
Pardon, Holmes?

HOLMES:
I merely wanted to demonstrate the absurdity of the suggestion that he let himself out of the tomb.

WATSON:
I see.

HOLMES:
He was dead all right. That body was stolen!

WATSON:
Stolen?

HOLMES:
Stolen, Watson. And the crime was either committed

by the occupying Romans, or the indigenous
Hebrews!

WATSON:

Of course!

HOLMES:

But the Romans have no wish to discredit their own
army.

WATSON:

Clearly not.

HOLMES:

So it must have been:

WATSON:

The Hebrews.

HOLMES:

Precisely!

WATSON:

Brilliant, Holmes! You've narrowed the field of sus-
pects to the entire Jewish nation. Which Hebrews in
particular?

HOLMES:

Very likely the temple authorities wishing to discredit
the followers of this man.

WATSON:

Very likely.

HOLMES:

No doubt they will shortly produce the body, and the
mystery will be solved.

WATSON:

No doubt.

    [Pause]

WATSON:

Holmes?

HOLMES:

Watson?

WATSON:
They've had nearly 2,000 years.
HOLMES:
Give them time, Watson.
    [*Pause*]
HOLMES:
[*Suddenly understanding*] Of course!
WATSON:
What?
HOLMES:
The disciples!
WATSON:
[*Looking around*] Where?
HOLMES:
They are the culprits.
WATSON:
They're the what?
HOLMES:
I shall reconstruct the scene. A group of desperate
men must steal a body in order to preserve their street
credibility.
    [*HOLMES and WATSON sneak towards the tomb*]
HOLMES:
But wait! The tomb is guarded. So they overpower the
sentries.
    [*HOLMES and WATSON sneak up behind imaginary
    sentries and mime hitting them on the head*]
HOLMES:
Push aside the stone ... [*HOLMES prepares to push
the stone, then has second thoughts*] Hardly a problem
for a dozen strong men. Then make off with the body,
and spread the story that Jesus has risen from the
dead!
WATSON:
All the time knowing that their story is a pack of lies!

HOLMES:
Of course!
WATSON:
But at the same time being prepared to risk their lives
telling people it's true!
    [*Pause*]
HOLMES:
Which is why the body of this man could not possibly
have been stolen by his followers.
WATSON:
So who moved the stone?
HOLMES:
Probably we will never know.

20

THE INTERROGATION

Scene:
  A police interrogation room, somewhere in Jerusalem, shortly after the resurrection. There is a chair for the interviewees to sit on, a DETECTIVE is pacing the room with a bundle of statements in his hand.

DETECTIVE:
[*Calling offstage*] All right, sergeant, send her in. [*Pause, as someone enters the room*] Ah! Sit down, dear. Mary Magdalene, is it? ... Good. Now, as you know, we are investigating the disappearance of a certain corpse, and I should just like to ask you a few questions, if I may ... Yes ... Yes, I know you gave us a statement. [*Indicating the papers*] I have it here in fact, but it is just a little obscure on one or two points, and I should like to tidy things up a bit, if I may.

[*Looking at the statement*] So, you have been acquainted with one, Jesus of Nazareth, for two and a half years, yes? ... And you were present at his execution? ... Fine. Now, the Sunday after the crucifixion you went to the tomb where it was your intention to embalm the body but, by the time you had arrived, the body had been removed. Now, this is the bit that gets me, Mary, because you see, you go on to say, [Reading] 'On leaving the tomb I saw the afore-mentioned Jesus of Nazareth in the garden outside and, not recognising him, asked him if he knew what had happened to the body.'

Now perhaps I'm just stupid or something, but, you must be the first person I've ever met who comes across a body lying in a garden, and starts chatting to it ... Oh, he wasn't lying down ... Yes, I can see it must have been very reassuring to see the two-day-old corpse of your best friend propped up against a tree ... He wasn't propped up against a tree. No, no, don't tell me, he was strolling across the hillside making daisy chains ... He wasn't making daisy chains.

Look Mary, you're a big girl now, and somebody really ought to tell you that dead bodies do not go for walks through gardens ... Oh, he wasn't dead? No, I don't suppose he would have been, do you? I mean, he had only been flogged, nailed to a cross, had a spear shoved in his side, and spent a quiet weekend in a sealed tomb. Yes, I expect he just woke up, felt like a bit of exercise and went for a stroll—I mean, the front door couldn't have weighed much more than about three-quarters of a ton. You know, it wouldn't sur-prise me if he was doing a spot of gardening when you met him ... You thought he was the gardener, did you? Mary, you were at that crucifixion, I was at that crucifixion—that man was not at all well when he was removed from that cross! ... Oh, he was dead, was he? Yes, of course that would explain why they put him in a tomb in the first place. All right, dear, run along. [He

watches her go] Deranged. [*He crumples the statement and drops it*]

[*Calling offstage again*] Right, sergeant, we'll have
Thomas back in again. [*He waits for Thomas to enter*]
Sit down lad. Now as far as I can see you're the only
sane one in this whole business. [*Leafing through
statements*] Peter, James, John, all having campfire
chats with dead carpenters ... Oh, you've got something new to tell me? So, going to come clean, are you?
Going to tell Uncle Cornelius what it is you've done
with the body? ... What do you mean it's not like that,
Thomas? ... Oh no, not you as well! [*Angrily*] Well,
don't think these little fairy tales of yours fool me, lad.
I wasn't born again yesterday, I know you took that
body ... Why? Well it's obvious isn't it? He was your
best mate, wasn't he? He said he'd rise from the dead.
You probably thought you could nick the body, bung
it some place else, and tell everybody he was back
from the dead. But seriously, Thomas, it never really
had a chance of coming off, did it? Now, why don't
you just tell us where you've put the body, and this
whole thing will blow over in a couple of months.
Well, you might get a few years on the galleys, but it's
not that bad—compared to what you're chancing—
look at what happened to your leader, that's what I
say. I mean, why risk your neck telling a story nobody
in their right mind's ever going to believe? Why?

21

A TOMB WITH A VIEW

Characters:
  JOSEPH OF ARIMATHEA well-meaning, but defensive
  MRS JOSEPH OF ARIMATHEA forthright, with a strong
  sense of propriety
  GARDENER
Scene:
  JOSEPH OF ARIMATHEA's house. He and his wife are
  arguing.

MRS JOSEPH:
[*Upset*] How could you?
JOSEPH:
I thought it was the right thing to do, under the
circumstances ...
MRS JOSEPH:
The right thing to do! To give away our family tomb to
this whatsisname from Nazareth.
JOSEPH:
His name's Jesus ...

MRS JOSEPH:

I don't care what his name is. What I care about is you giving away our tomb without telling me.

JOSEPH:

I'm telling you now.

MRS JOSEPH:

Well it's a bit late now, isn't it?

JOSEPH:

There wasn't time before.

MRS JOSEPH:

You could have made the time.

JOSEPH:

So what was I supposed to do? Bring the body back here and say, 'What do you think about giving this chap a berth in the family grave?'?

MRS JOSEPH:

I just don't see why you had to get involved.

JOSEPH:

Because he needed a tomb.

MRS JOSEPH:

We need a tomb!

JOSEPH:

Not as much as he does.

MRS JOSEPH:

How come?

JOSEPH:

Because he's dead.

MRS JOSEPH:

We'll be dead too some day—what are we going to do, then?

JOSEPH:

Not a lot, I should think.

MRS JOSEPH:

You just don't take me seriously, do you? Sometimes I wonder why I married you, Joseph of Arimathea.

JOSEPH:

[*Gently*] Look I'm sorry if I've upset you, but what's done is done, we can always get another tomb.

MRS JOSEPH:

But that one was special.

JOSEPH:

I know it meant a lot to you ...

MRS JOSEPH:

It should have meant a lot to you, as well. It was a wedding present.

JOSEPH:

Only your mother would give somebody a tomb as a wedding present.

MRS JOSEPH:

Don't talk about my mother in that tone of voice!

JOSEPH:

Sorry.

MRS JOSEPH:

It was very thoughtful of her.

JOSEPH:

I'm sure it was, but I really didn't know what to say when she led us out to see it. 'Thanks, just what we needed'? or 'I can't wait to try it out'?

MRS JOSEPH:

Well, anything would have been better than what you did say.

JOSEPH:

Let's not go over that again.

MRS JOSEPH:

You told her she was welcome to use it any time she liked.

JOSEPH:

All I meant was ...

MRS JOSEPH:

I know what you meant. You never did like my family, did you?

JOSEPH:
Look, there's plenty of room left ...

MRS JOSEPH:
Are you seriously suggesting that we could still use it?

JOSEPH:
I don't see why not.

MRS JOSEPH:
Over my dead body! That man was a common criminal!

JOSEPH:
Nonsense!

MRS JOSEPH:
Then why was he executed?

JOSEPH:
Those were trumped-up charges.

MRS JOSEPH:
Are you one of his followers as well?

JOSEPH:
I just found a lot of things he said interesting.

MRS JOSEPH:
Interesting! The man was off his head!

JOSEPH:
He wasn't.

MRS JOSEPH:
He said he was the Messiah. If those aren't delusions of grandeur, I don't know what are.

JOSEPH:
Perhaps he was the Messiah.

MRS JOSEPH:
Then why couldn't he afford his own tomb?
        [GARDENER *knocks and enters*]

GARDENER:
Excuse me?

MRS JOSEPH:
Yes?

GARDENER:
I'm looking for Mr and Mrs Joseph of Arimathea.
JOSEPH:
Yes.
GARDENER:
I'm from Gethsemane Garden Maintenance, we take care of the plot outside your tomb and I'm afraid your account's overdue.
MRS JOSEPH:
[*To* JOSEPH] Typical! Full of grand gestures but too busy to pay your bills.
JOSEPH:
[*Fumbling with his chequebook*] Look, here's a cheque ... [*He starts writing out a cheque*]
MRS JOSEPH:
[*To* GARDENER] We won't be needing your services any more.
GARDENER:
Aren't you satisfied with us?
MRS JOSEPH:
Oh, it's nothing to do with you—I'm quite satisfied with you. It's my husband I'm not satisfied with, giving away our tomb to a stranger.
GARDENER:
[*Embarrassed*] Ah!
JOSEPH:
[*Handing* GARDENER *a cheque*] There.
MRS JOSEPH:
It was such a nice tomb. Don't you think?
GARDENER:
As tombs go.
MRS JOSEPH:
It was lovely. And now it belongs to somebody else.
JOSEPH:
Ahem! Well, I'm sure this gentleman's very busy ...

MRS JOSEPH:
Don't interrupt! [To GARDENER] What would you do?

GARDENER:
Ask for it back, I suppose.

MRS JOSEPH:
It's a bit late for that—he's dead already.

GARDENER:
[Puzzled] Oh, so where is he now?

MRS JOSEPH:
What do you mean 'Where is he?'? He's in the tomb.

GARDENER:
In your tomb?

MRS JOSEPH:
Doesn't anybody ever listen to a single word I say? Of course he's in our tomb.

GARDENER:
I'm just surprised I didn't see him there this morning.

JOSEPH:
Well, you wouldn't have been able to with the rock across the entrance.

GARDENER:
But there wasn't any rock across the entrance.

JOSEPH:
Yes there was!

GARDENER:
No there wasn't.

JOSEPH:
There was!

GARDENER:
There wasn't.

JOSEPH:
There must have been. I put it there!

GARDENER:
I'm afraid there wasn't. And as far as I could see, the tomb looked pretty empty too. Now, if you'll

excuse me, I really must be getting along. [GARDENER
leaves]

MRS JOSEPH:

[*Delighted*] Our tomb's empty again.

JOSEPH:

[*Bewildered*] It must have been grave-robbers.

MRS JOSEPH:

[*Ignoring* JOSEPH] Empty!

JOSEPH:

[*Ignoring* MRS JOSEPH] Grave-robbers!

MRS JOSEPH:

No nasty strangers cluttering it up.

JOSEPH:

I just don't understand how they got past the guards.

MRS JOSEPH:

Now we can use it any time we like.

JOSEPH:

But he could hardly have let himself out, could he?

MRS JOSEPH:

Our wedding tomb.

JOSEPH:

Could he?

MRS JOSEPH:

It's got such a lovely view.

'HE WAS DEAD, I'M POSITIVE...'

22

HILLSIDE STORY

For children, indoors. Read Appendix 3, 'Working with Children', before using this sketch. Alternatively, it may be performed by adults as a street-theatre item.

Characters:
  NARRATOR   played by adult
  OFFICER   typical sergeant-major type, should be played by the NARRATOR
  CROWD of SOLDIERS/GRASS   minimum of four
Scene:
  Outside the tomb where Jesus was buried. No set is required; the only essential prop is a sheet. At the start, the stage is empty apart from the NARRATOR. If there are more than four children, ignore the numbering and let them take it in turns to speak.

NARRATOR:
The story is set on a hillside. And on that hillside is a garden.
  [CROWD, *who are offstage, make garden sounds: birds singing, leaves rustling, etc*]

129

NARRATOR:
And in that garden was a cave. And in front of that cave was some grass.

> [CROWD *runs onstage, and each person becomes a blade of* GRASS]

NARRATOR:
Some people had put a body in that cave.

1ST GRASS:
[Sniffs] What's that smell?

2ND GRASS:
It's a body.

3RD GRASS:
They can't just leave it there.

4TH GRASS:
It'll smell awful.

NARRATOR:
And they put a big rock across the entrance—on top of the grass!

> [GRASS *all crumple to the floor and groan, as if a great weight has just been placed on top of them*]

1ST GRASS:
What did they do that for?

2ND GRASS:
How would they like a rock on their heads!

3RD GRASS:
Owww! My back!

4TH GRASS:
Never mind your back, what about my head?

NARRATOR:
Then after a while, the rock was taken away again.

1ST GRASS:
What a relief.

2ND GRASS:
Glad that's over.

3RD GRASS:

What a nice bright day.

4TH GRASS:

But it's the middle of the night.

1ST GRASS:

Then where's all this light coming from?

2ND GRASS:

That man's coming out of the cave.

3RD GRASS:

I thought he was dead.

4TH GRASS:

Well, he isn't now, is he?

NARRATOR:

In that same garden, not far from the cave, were some soldiers.

[GRASS *become* SOLDIERS. *They indicate this by standing to attention and saluting*]

NARRATOR:

They were supposed to be guarding the cave, but they'd all fallen asleep.

[SOLDIERS *collapse to the floor and start snoring*]

NARRATOR:

When the commanding officer arrived in the morning, and saw that the stone had been moved, he wasn't very pleased.

[NARRATOR *now becomes* OFFICER *and strides into the middle of the sleeping* SOLDIERS]

OFFICER:

What is going on here?

[SOLDIERS *wake up and look guilty. They stand in a line to attention*]

OFFICER:

You were supposed to be guarding the cave.

[SOLDIERS *nod*]

OFFICER:
It's been robbed!

    [SOLDIERS *look shocked*]

OFFICER:
Who's idea was it to catch a bit of shut-eye, then?

1ST SOLDIER:
[*Pointing at someone else*] He went to sleep before I did.

2ND SOLDIER:
[*Pointing at another* SOLDIER] No, I didn't, he did.

3RD SOLDIER:
[*Pointing at yet another* SOLDIER] You fibber, I was the last one awake, he started it ...

OFFICER:
QUIET!

4TH SOLDIER:
[*Pointing at someone else*] He started it!

ALL SOLDIERS:
[*Together, at the one who has just spoken*] Sssh!

OFFICER:
Well, you can start by searching the cave for clues.

    [SOLDIERS *start to march off and take up positions as* GRASS *again. The* OFFICER *goes back to being the* NARRATOR]

NARRATOR:
The grass in front of the cave was feeling very pleased with itself.

    [GRASS *looks self-satisfied*]

NARRATOR:
The sun was shining, the rock had gone. It was a good day for grass. Then, all of a sudden, fifteen Roman soldiers came running into the cave!

1ST GRASS:
Look out!

    [GRASS *acts as if it is being trampled on*]

2ND GRASS:
What did they do that for?

NARRATOR:
And it had just about recovered when the soldiers came running back again!

3RD GRASS:
Here they come again!

[GRASS *is trampled on again*]

NARRATOR: -
And while the grass was feeling even sorrier for itself than before, the soldiers were reporting back.

[GRASS *become* SOLDIERS *again, and one of them collects a sheet from the side of the stage. They stand in a line to attention.* NARRATOR *becomes* OFFICER *again*]

1ST SOLDIER:
Search of the cave completed, sir!

OFFICER:
Did you find anything?

1ST SOLDIER:
Just this shroud. [*Hands sheet to* OFFICER]

OFFICER: [*Looks at sheet*] We'll send that to the forensic lab at Turin. [*Throws it aside*] Anything else?

[SOLDIERS *shake their heads*]

OFFICER:
What am I supposed to tell the Colonel?

2ND SOLDIER:
That the body escaped, sir.

OFFICER:
That a dead body got past fifteen Roman soldiers? Don't be stupid!

3RD SOLDIER:
That it was stolen, sir.

OFFICER:
Stolen by whom?

4TH SOLDIER:
I don't know, I was asleep.

1ST SOLDIER:
So was I.

2ND SOLDIER:
Me too.

OFFICER:
Well, use your imagination.

3RD SOLDIER:
Maybe it was the Hebrews, sir.

OFFICER:
They were the ones who asked us to guard it.

4TH SOLDIER:
Maybe it was the Romans.

ALL SOLDIERS:
[*Together*] We are the Romans!

    [OFFICER *goes back to being* NARRATOR, *and* SOLDIERS
    go back to being GRASS]

NARRATOR:
And so they kept on arguing about what had happened. Of course, the grass knew.

1ST GRASS:
You mean he came back to life?

2ND GRASS:
That's right.

3RD GRASS:
I didn't think people could do that.

4TH GRASS:
Well, this one did, didn't he?

NARRATOR:
But I don't suppose anybody thought to ask the grass.

23

THE PUBLISHER

Scene:
The EDITOR's office at the Jerusalem University Press. The EDITOR is sitting behind a desk with a manuscript in his hands. He stands to greet someone who has just entered the room.

EDITOR:
John! John, come in. Take a seat. John, when the Jerusalem University Press asked you to do a biography of the Galilean Carpenter, what we had in mind was, well, a biography really. Something that would help us get to grips with the man behind the public face, something that would demythologise him, something that would explain him. [*Picking up the manuscript*] So what's this? Fifty pages of theology. You haven't given us any background, his upbringing, his early career, nothing. You haven't even told us his father's name ... Please John, can we keep God out of this for just a moment.

Now, what I suggest we do is run through the manuscript together and I'll show you where we want a bit more detail, then you can go and rework those sections. [*Looking at the manuscript*] Now, ah yes, the title. Now you've called it a Gospel, that's just what I mean by too much theology. You really can't have that sort of editorial comment on the front cover. I suggest something snappier—*A Prophet Lost*—that kind of thing.

[*Reading*] Opening section, poetic, a bit obscure but that's all right. After all, we are an academic publisher. Ah, now the first problem—the arrival of Jesus. You've told us about John the Baptist telling people to repent and flinging them in the Jordan and, all of a sudden, in walks Jesus, a fully grown man. What we need here is a section on his early life, those formative years before he took the street-preaching scene by storm ... What do you mean, it's not relevant, of course it's relevant. Background's always relevant. Or are you suggesting that he was the perfect child? ... I see. Right, well, let's move on.

Now, all these so-called 'miracles'. We've got water into wine, we've got invalids walking, we've got the dead being raised! But there's never a single word of explanation. Now the whole point of this book is to get at the man behind the myth ... Well of course you say they're not myths, but you never back anything up. I mean, this business of feeding, what, 5,000 people with a few fishpaste sandwiches, we've only got your word on that ... and the 5,000 others, I grant you. But what about the man himself? Where's the gentle Jesus meek and mild, the man who sat children on his knee and told people to be nice to one another? Never even gets a mention.

You've described some lunatic who goes around telling people that if they eat his body they'll live for ever—so long as they can arrange to be born again first. I thought you were one of his friends! ... And will you stop bringing God into it—the religious department is at the other end of the corridor. I deal with biographies, with hard facts, and I wouldn't have thought this one was that difficult.

Look at the source material. Here's a man, a simple tradesman from a provincial backwater. Five years ago nobody had heard of him, and suddenly he's national news, people turn out in droves to hear him, the authorities don't like it, they try to stop him, but he's just too popular; for three years he travels round the country, never stopping anywhere for more than a few weeks, always at the centre of some controversy, then at last he makes his triumphal entry into Jerusalem —cheering crowds line the streets, they hail him like a returning king, the world is at his feet! Within forty-eight hours he's been arrested, tried and executed, cut down in his prime, betrayed by one of his closest friends.

This is the stuff of epic fiction, and it actually happened in our lifetime. You saw it first hand, and what do you come up with? A tract.

I'm sorry, John, but we're a respected publishing house and if you're not prepared to change it. I'm afraid there's nothing I can do for you. But I do think you've got a lot of potential, and if you come up with anything else I'd like to see it. Anything in the pipeline? ... Revelation, good title. Well, drop it by when it's finished and I'll take a look, but—one word of advice—if you want us to take it seriously, try to make it a bit more down to earth.

'WHAT WAS THE FATHER'S NAME?...'

24

THE SILLY SEASON

Characters:

MARCUS   cynical newspaper hack
GAIUS   similar
LUCIUS   enthusiastic young journalist
JOURNALIST   runs in at the end

Scene:

Newsroom of the *Daily Citizen*. There are three desks, a telephone on each. MARCUS is at his desk, speaking on the phone. GAIUS sits at his desk, staring into space. The third desk is empty.

MARCUS:

... Uhu. And whereabouts did you see these water-melons? ... Hovering over the Coliseum, right. Where were you at the time? ... Ah, I see, and was it a good party? ... Of course I don't think you imagined it ... Yes, I'm sure it was a very sober gathering, and then you saw this flock of water-melons over the Coliseum. Did you see anything else? ... Oh, I don't know, a few gooseberries maybe, an olive? ... Yes, I know, I'm being silly. Well, we'll look into it as soon as we can, but we're dreadfully busy at the moment ... Yes, if your story's confirmed, you'll certainly get your picture in the paper [MARCUS *hangs up*].

GAIUS:

Another great exclusive, eh, Marcus?

MARCUS:

Why isn't there any news in Rome?

GAIUS:

It's the silly season, Marcus. The Emperor's left the city for his summer residence, the chariot races are over until the autumn, and there isn't another circus for four weeks.

MARCUS:

There must be something going on.

[LUCIUS *enters briskly with a sheaf of papers under his arm*]

LUCIUS:

Morning! [LUCIUS *goes to his desk and starts working*]

GAIUS:

[*Suspiciously*] Morning, Lucius. What have you got there? [GAIUS *gets up and moves towards* LUCIUS's *desk*]

LUCIUS:

[*Unconvincingly*] Oh, nothing much.

[GAIUS *tries to peer over* LUCIUS's *shoulder, who tries elaborately to conceal what he is doing*]

GAIUS:

What's it about?

LUCIUS:

Nothing.

GAIUS:

Then you won't mind if I have a look ... [GAIUS *tries to take some of* LUCIUS's *papers*]

LUCIUS:

[*Sharply*] Yes, I do mind actually. Now could we talk later, I'm rather busy at the moment.

GAIUS:

OK.

> [GAIUS *and* MARCUS *look at each other.* GAIUS *nods at* MARCUS's *phone;* MARCUS *smiles and lifts the receiver*]

MARCUS:

Hello? Oh Lucius, it's for you.

LUCIUS:

Oh, thanks.

> [LUCIUS *walks over to* MARCUS's *desk and picks up the phone; meanwhile,* GAIUS *picks up* LUCIUS's *papers*]

LUCIUS:

Hello? Hello? There's no one there.

> [LUCIUS *turns and sees what* GAIUS *is doing*]

LUCIUS:

Leave those alone!

GAIUS:

So who's Jesus of Nazareth?

LUCIUS:

None of your business.

GAIUS:

[*Reading*] Native of Judea. Where's Judea, Marcus?

MARCUS:

Never heard of it.

LUCIUS:

It's one of the eastern provinces. Now will you give those back!

> [LUCIUS *strides over to* GAIUS, *who throws the papers over to* MARCUS]

GAIUS:

What do you think, Marcus?

MARCUS:

[*Reading*] Didn't get on with the authorities, did he? Subversive, delusions of grandeur. Might be something in it.

[*LUCIUS goes to MARCUS and snatches the papers back*]

LUCIUS:

That's enough!

MARCUS:

[*Defensively*] Just interested, Lucius.

LUCIUS:

Interested in pinching my story.

MARCUS:

Lucius! How could you think such a thing!

GAIUS:

Surely you know us better than that?

LUCIUS:

Hmph!

[*LUCIUS goes back to his desk; he picks up the phone and starts dialling. MARCUS and GAIUS both grab their own phones and dial as well*]

GAIUS:

Directory?

MARCUS:

Information?

GAIUS:

Get me the governor of Judea!

MARCUS:

What have you got on Jesus of Nazareth?

LUCIUS:

Hello, is that John? ... I understand you were a friend of Jesus of Nazareth ...

MARCUS:

Jesus of Nazareth, he's big news in ... um ...

GAIUS:

The Governor of Judea!

MARCUS:

Judea, that's the place. Somewhere out east.

LUCIUS:

No, John, I'm nothing to do with the police, I'm a

journalist with the *Daily Citizen* ... It's not a gutter rag!

MARCUS:

OK, try religious leaders. Find me a Chief Priest or somebody.

GAIUS:

Governor Pilate? ... A great privilege, sir, I wonder what you could tell me about Jesus of Nazareth?

LUCIUS:

Could you be a bit more specific, John—the son of which God?

MARCUS:

High Priest's Office? ... Very grateful for your time. I wonder if you could give me some information on Jesus of Nazareth. [MARCUS *holds the phone away from his ear, as if he is being shouted at*] I take it, you didn't get on too well?

GAIUS:

So, Governor, why was he executed?

LUCIUS:

Hang on, John—you say he performed miracles?

GAIUS:

[*Taking notes*] He travelled round the country gathering support ...

MARCUS:

What do you mean, he claimed to be more than human?

LUCIUS:

And how would you explain these miracles?

GAIUS:

[*Still taking notes*] Had twelve senior lieutenants known as 'the disciples' ...

LUCIUS:

Can we keep God out of this for a moment ...

MARCUS:

And where does the heavenly father bit fit in?

GAIUS:
Sounds pretty subversive to me, sir.

MARCUS:
He said his heavenly father sent him to earth?

GAIUS:
So he claimed to be some kind of king ...

LUCIUS:
You'll have to try and back up some of these miracles, John ...

MARCUS:
Did he ever explicitly state that he was a spaceman?

GAIUS:
And they cheered him when he rode into the capital?

LUCIUS:
This feeding business—how many witnesses have you got? ... 5,000, eh?

MARCUS:
Told a lot of stories about sheep ...

GAIUS:
Sounds like treason to me, sir.

LUCIUS:
What about some quotes—some of the things he said?

MARCUS:
He called himself the good shepherd ...

GAIUS:
They worship him after his death ...

MARCUS:
And accused you of being wolves in sheep's clothing ...

GAIUS:
All sounds very nasty, sir.

MARCUS:
Would you say he was obsessed by sheep?

LUCIUS:
And he said all this after he came back from the dead?

MARCUS:
Well, I think I've got enough there.

GAIUS:
Good of you to spare the time.

LUCIUS:
Thanks for all your help.

MARCUS
GAIUS } Goodbye.
LUCIUS

GAIUS:
[*To MARCUS*] What did you get?

MARCUS:
[*Reading from notes*] 'Mad Spaceman with Sheep Fetish Upsets Religious Zealots'. How about you?

GAIUS:
[*Reading*] 'Revolutionary Perishes, but Sinister Death-Cult Lives on'. What about you, Lucius?

LUCIUS:
I knew you were going to pinch it!

MARCUS:
Oh, come on!

LUCIUS:
[*Reading*] 'Son of God Executed, but Enjoys Speedy Recovery'.

MARCUS:
[*To GAIUS*] What do you reckon?

GAIUS:
All sounds a bit far-fetched to me.

    [*JOURNALIST runs in*]

JOURNALIST:
There's been another sighting of the water-melons. They're over the Coliseum now!

GAIUS:
This is more like it—a real news story!

    [*THEY ALL RUN OFF*]

APPENDIX 1

Using the Sketches

Before using any of these scripts you should remember: there is no such thing as an actor-proof sketch. Any of the material in this book can fall hopelessly flat. It's up to you to make sure it doesn't. Some ways of doing this are outlined below.

The first question to ask is, 'Why are we doing it?' Are you trying to brighten up an ordinary service? Do you want to make a particular evangelistic point? Or is it just because the vicar asked you? If you don't have a reason, don't do it. Part of the motivation should always be the enthusiasm of the performers— if they're bored, the audience will be too—but this must not be the only reason. Don't go foisting sketches on an unwilling congregation.

The next thing to consider is the physical environment. Look at the space you're going to use and work within it. If the acoustics are dreadful and you can only be heard with microphones, use them. If the only microphones available are on stands that can't be moved, do a sketch that doesn't require much movement. If you're working on the street, allow for the noise and the interruptions, and use sketches where people can afford not to hear all the words. Where sketches are particularly suitable for children or for street-theatre, I have said so, but you still need to use your own judgement and common sense.

Another important factor is the audience. If it's a quiet Sunday-evening congregation, 'The Silly Season' is probably not appropriate; if, on the other hand, it's the members of a local youth club, 'The Garden' is unlikely to captivate them. Also bear in mind many of the scripts in this book presuppose a certain amount of biblical knowledge which some people may lack.

Finally, before starting to rehearse, make sure that the sketch is going to fit in with the rest of the programme. In the case of a church service, you can ensure this by talking to the minister beforehand and showing him a copy of the script. If it's a larger event, involving outside speakers for instance, get in touch with them, find out what they are going to be saying, and try to work around them. If this proves difficult— either you can't get in touch, or the information you get is too vague—at least make sure that they know what you plan to do.

Once you've done all this, you can get down to rehearsing. It is critical that any public performance is properly rehearsed which will usually require between two and four hours per sketch. It sounds like a lot of time—it is—but to spend any less is to show a casual disregard for the audience.

In the past I've found it most useful to hold two rehearsals of between one and two hours in the week preceding the performance. If you have a group that already meets regularly, this can be modified, but in any event you will need to work on the script at least twice: once with books, once when everybody has learned their lines. Although there are no rules for rehearsing, the following ideas have been useful to me in the past:

1   Start, and especially finish, on time. If everybody knows there is a limited period available, less time will be wasted.

2   Appoint a director. Groups of people have a tendency to discuss things for ever rather than make a decision. The job of the director is not to take absolute control of the proceedings, but to make decisions when things grind to a halt, and generally keep the whole process moving.

3   Have one or two read-throughs to decide on the parts. Again, don't agonise for too long over this. If it's really that difficult to decide who does what, it probably isn't going to make that much difference anyway.

4   Start 'blocking' as soon as possible. 'Blocking' is the posh theatrical word for telling people where to stand when they say their lines, and where some kind of direction is essential. Before starting this, it's helpful to mark out the area in which you're going to perform.

5   Have a run-through to see what the blocking looks like, and tidy up the parts that don't work.

6   Now, and only now, start looking at the way it is being performed. This is where everybody gets the chance to start acting!

If you're trying to get by on the minimum two rehearsals, make sure that you get at least as far as point 5 at the first one. If there's time to do more, so much the better; it will make it easier for people to learn their lines.

As far as the staging of the sketch goes (ie how the

furniture is arranged, what props are used, and so on), this should be decided no later than stage 4, and it can save time if the director comes with some fairly clear ideas.

Now, some 'don'ts':

1   Don't worry excessively about 'giving everybody a shot' (not always applicable to children; see Appendix 3). People should play parts because they are capable, not because they might be offended at being left out. Always remember the performance is for the benefit of the audience, and they have a right to the best you can offer. In addition I'd suggest that those with talents should be encouraged, not passed over in favour of the over-sensitive.

2   Don't leave people undirected to 'do what feels natural' on stage; it will have the opposite effect. There is nothing natural about standing in front of a crowd of perhaps several hundred people and talking as if they weren't there.

3   Don't keep letting people off the hook for not knowing their lines in rehearsal. When you're in front of an audience, remembering lines is harder, not easier.

The suggestions I've made here are not designed to remove the pleasure from performing. On the contrary, I find that when the actors are well-rehearsed, sure of what they are doing individually, and confident that they won't let each other down, performing is at its most exciting, most effective, and most fun.

APPENDIX 2

Monologues

The great attraction of monologues is that you can do them on your own. Rehearsing is easy—you just pick up the book and rehearse—you don't need to worry about anybody else, you just learn your lines, work out your moves, and do it on the night. Follow these straightforward instructions and you can quite easily embarrass yourself in front of an entire congregation.

Monologues are far more demanding than most other types of sketch, and if anything goes wrong, you're on your own. This appendix deals with the peculiar difficulties of rehearsing this kind of script. However, before getting on to the details of rehearsing, I should explain some of the conventions I've used in the scripts.

First of all, I haven't included many directions. This doesn't mean I intend them all to be performed by a motionless actor talking directly to the audience; it means that you have to decide how to perform them yourself. Remember that decisions must be made. It's very uncomfortable to watch a performer who is uncertain about what he or she is doing.

Where another character is speaking I have put in a dotted line. The actor should have a clear idea of what the missing lines are. I haven't written them in because it would clutter up the page—once again the decisions are yours.

The first major difficulty with rehearsing a monologue is that it can be boring—opportunities for chatting with the cast are clearly limited—and for this reason rehearsals can fizzle out before they ever get started. To get around this problem, I would suggest taking the following steps:

1 Go into a room by yourself and switch off televisions, radios, record players, or anything else that might distract you.
2 Unless the directions state otherwise, stand in the middle of the room and start reading the script out loud.
3 Read through the script two or three times stressing different words, using various tones of voice, and pausing in different places.
4 Once you've found a tone of voice you're happy with, think about when you might sit or move around the stage.
5 Stop after 45 minutes.

It's quite likely that you won't be entirely satisfied after one session, in which case pick up at the next one where you left off. To rehearse in this way takes a great .deal of concentration, and it's unlikely that you'll be achieving much after an hour. I would add the following 'don'ts':

1 Don't mumble quietly to yourself: speak as you intend to speak in performance, otherwise it doesn't count as proper rehearsing.

2 Don't go overboard on different accents. They're far more difficult than most people imagine, and since your voice is the only one the audience will hear, it has to be convincing.

3 Don't make lots of moves around the stage. All the monologues are quite short, and people don't move around much in a five-minute conversation.

Once you've been through this lot, you should ask someone whose judgement you trust to direct you. If you can't find anybody, I would question whether you should be doing the sketch at all. At any event, it is essential that somebody else should see you go through the sketch before you perform it in public, otherwise you put yourself under far too much pressure on the night and disaster is almost inevitable.

Assuming you do find someone to help, have been through the preliminaries, and are reasonably familiar with the script, I'd suggest managing the 'directed' rehearsals as follows:

1 Go through what you have done so far in front of the director.

2 Discuss any major changes of tone or delivery, and try them out immediately. It's much better to have a go than spend ages arguing about what might or might not work.

3 Once any drastic alterations have been made, go through the whole sketch again, stopping to adjust things as you go along.

4 Go through the whole sketch without stopping. At the end, the director should give notes outlining any mistakes or further changes required.

5 Carry on alternating 'stopping runs' and 'runs' until you are satisfied, but, in any case:

6 Stop after an hour.

At this stage you should learn your lines, and the best way I've found of doing this is to put down the book and go through the words in your head. If you get stuck, look at the script long enough to get going again, then carry on as before. It's quite a good idea to go through your lines silently on buses, trains and in supermarkets, because if you can remember them there, you can probably remember them anywhere. Being able to get through them in a silent room with no distractions doesn't mean you'll get through them in performance.

The minimum number of rehearsals you can manage with is three. One to familiarise yourself with the script, one with a director, and one more, preferably with the director again, after you know your lines. The final rehearsal can be quite short, perhaps only twenty or thirty minutes, and should consist mainly of uninterrupted runs with notes at the end.

The monologues in this book are simple in as much as they require minimal props and set. They aren't simple to perform, and should only be done by people who are fairly experienced. A badly performed monologue is a joyless occasion for audience and performer alike, and unlike other kinds of sketch, if a monologue sinks, you go down alone.

APPENDIX 3

Working with Children

When adults are performing, the hope is that the audience will be informed; when children are performing, the object is more often to teach those taking part. This is an important distinction, and a quite different approach to rehearsing is required in each case.

Before outlining how rehearsals should be run, however, it's worth explaining how the scripts work. They all contain an 'anchor-part' of two or three roles which should be taken by an adult, and a large number of other lines to be shared out evenly between the children. The object of this is to have one person on stage at all times who can control the pace, leaving the children with equally sized parts.

To work on one of them some kind of peace and quiet is required—if there are people playing football and throwing paint around in the same room, it will be almost impossible to concentrate. Assuming you have a suitable venue, here are some useful guidelines:

1 Approach the sessions enthusiastically. Apathy is infectious, and not at all conducive to good behaviour.

2 Give firm directions. In order to do this, some preparation is essential, even if it's only fifteen minutes the night before.

3 Encourage the children to make suggestions of their own, but don't feel obliged to include every one. Children are much better at handling artistic criticism than adults.

4 Be as fair as possible in sharing out lines. Failure to do this is almost guaranteed to cause upset.

5 Ensure that the rehearsals do lead to a performance. Although this is not the ultimate object from your point of view, the children will feel cheated without it.

These are all fairly general remarks. The problem of what to do with your roomful of noisy kids remains. Assuming you have decided what sketch to use, how you are going to direct it, and who the audience will be, this is how I would begin:

1 Start with a game, preferably one that has more to do with concentration than running around. Possibilities include:

Murder Winks: all stand in a circle facing inwards; a 'detective' is nominated, and leaves the room while the 'murderer' is chosen. The detective then stands in the middle of the circle and tries to find the murderer. The murderer 'kills' people by winking at them, and they should 'die' as dramatically as possible.

Pass the Thing: a 'neutral' object like a box or a stick is passed around a circle and everybody has to mime a different use for it. For example, the stick could be a toothbrush, a golf club, or a large pencil.

A variation on this is for the leader to say 'Pass it as if it was ...' (a snake, a priceless vase, burning hot, etc).

Storytelling: the leader tells the first sentence of a story, and the next person in the circle has to continue. The leader signals, and it passes on to the next person, and so on, all the way round the circle.

2   Explain to the children where they are to imagine the audience sitting. Don't explain the plot; it's much better if they find that out for themselves.

3   Position the children wherever you want them for the beginning of the sketch. Stand where the audience will be and direct from there. So long as you have done some preparation, and have an idea of your own moves, your part can be fitted in later.

4   Start 'narrating' and break out of the lines to give directions. For instance, in Sketch 22 'Hillside Story', begin: 'The story is set on a hillside, and on that hillside was a garden.' Then spend two or three minutes arranging some garden sounds.

5   Go back over the same section, but this time let the children do their garden sounds 'on cue'. Don't worry if they're not very good; carry on and come back to that part later. It's most important that the plot keeps moving or people will start to become bored.

6   Continue narrating until the children have another action, then stop and work on it as before. Don't keep going all the way back to the beginning or the whole process will come to a standstill.

7   When issuing lines, simply tell the children what to say and have them repeat the words back to you; don't go passing around scripts or books. Lines should be given out on a rotational basis wherever possible.

8   At the end of a session, go through everything you have done so far.

9   Once you have been all the way through a script
and are reasonably satisfied with the way it looks, slot
in your own moves.

This is a slow process—it will take between two and
four hours to rehearse one sketch—but there is no way
round it. If you're looking for something that can be
prepared in under an hour, you limit yourself to about
1½ minutes of plot, or something so simple that it
contains no interest for the children.

Should you decide to use one of these sketches, you
will therefore need three or four rehearsals, probably
spread over a number of different days. Because of the
way they are written, it's not essential to have exactly
the same people every time—a turnover of two or
three people per rehearsal will only mean reallocating
half a dozen lines—but it's best if you have a reasonably consistent group.

The sketches contained here are not ideal for every
situation, and there is no reason why you shouldn't
try to write your own, but be warned—if rehearsing
seems slow, writing is almost stationary. Although,
like most people, I can produce rubbish impressively
fast, I generally reckon on spending around two hours
per minute of usable script produced. If you think you
can do better, good luck!